Summer Bridge A

M000106191

 Canadian Style!

Second to Third Grade

SBA was created by	written by	exercise illustrations by
Michele D. Van Leeuwen	**Julia Ann Hobbs** **Carla Dawn Fisher**	**Amanda Sorensen**

This Workbook Contains:

 Fun, skill-based activities in reading, writing, arithmetic, and language arts with additional activities in geography and science to keep your child busy, happy, and learning! *Summer Bridge Activities*™❋ was designed specifically for Canadian school children and is based on content from the original best-selling **Summer Bridge Activities**™ series. *Summer Bridge Activities*™❋ is divided into three sections for review and preview, with pages numbered by day. Children complete their work quickly with the easy-to-use format, leaving lots of time for play!

 A Summer Reading List based on the Accelerated Reader Program.

 Incentive Contracts to encourage summer learning and reward your child's efforts. "Discover Something New" lists of creative things to do are found on the back side of each *Summer Bridge Activities*™❋ Incentive Contract Calendar for when your child asks the inevitable: "What can I do? I'm bored."

 Comprehensive Word Lists, which contain words to sound, read, and spell, challenge children and encourage them to build their vocabulary. *Summer Bridge Activities*™❋ 2–3 also contains Addition and Subtraction Flashcards, 0 to 18.

 Tear-Out Answer Pages to help correct your child's work.

 An official Certificate of Completion to be awarded for successfully completing the workbook.

Mr. Fredrickson

Ms. Hansen

Here are some groups who think our books are great!

Hey Kids and Parents!
Log on to
summerbridgeactivities.com
for more eye-boggling,
mind-bending, brain-twisting
summer fun!
www.summerbridgeactivities.com

Summer Bridge Activities™ ✦ Canadian Style!
2nd to 3rd Grade

Rainbow Bridge Publishing thanks those involved in the creation of this book:

Kathleen Bratcher, Clareen Arnold, Andy Carlson, Suzie Ellison, Robyn Funk,
Randy Harward, Jerold Johnson, Zack Johnson, Kristina Kugler, Molly McMahon,
Dante J. Orazzi, Paul Rawlins, Amanda Sorensen, George Starks,
Michele D. Van Leeuwen, Scott G. Van Leeuwen, Jennifer Willes

Please visit our website at
www.summerbridgeactivities.com/canada
for supplements, additions, and corrections to this book.

Second Edition 2004

ISBN: 1-887923-39-X

Table of Contents

Dear Parents,

Choosing Summer Bridge Activities™✸ to help reinforce classroom skills clearly shows that you believe education is important and valuable. Your involvement is vital to your child's immediate and long-term academic success. No matter how wonderful your child's classroom experience is, it needs to be reinforced so that it will not be forgotten.

It is important not to overwhelm your child with just academics. Your child also should be encouraged to enjoy a variety of recreational and cultural activities outside the classroom, but reinforcing academic skills can and should be enjoyable. Summer Bridge Activities™✸ is a great tool to help you do both!

Let me tell you why Summer Bridge Activities™✸ was originally created. As a parent of a first grader, summer was quickly approaching. I was concerned that the skills he had worked so hard to develop would be forgotten if I did not do something to support them. I was apprehensive about his adjustment to school after three months of play and wanted to help in any way I could.

I spoke with his teacher, other school administrators, and parents and found I was not alone with my concerns. I was told by several educators that up to 80% of what children are taught in school can be lost, unless that knowledge is reinforced quickly and continuously! I certainly did not want this to happen to my son!

I looked for appropriate workbooks but could not find any that correlated with curriculum guidelines in an easy-to-use format. So, as a concerned parent, I organized a team of award-winning teachers and informed educators to create a series of workbooks that would make reviewing classroom skills, including reading, writing, arithmetic, geography, and language arts, fun and rewarding. Welcome to Summer Bridge Activities™✸!

Thank you for choosing this wonderful program to assist with your child's academic success. I wish you the best of luck in helping your child get the most out of his education. Also, we welcome you to **www.summerbridgeactivities.com**, where you will find fun, interactive summer learning games, ideas, and activities for you and your child at no additional cost! We look forward to seeing you there! Have a great summer and happy learning!

Sincerely,

Michele D. Van Leeuwen

Michele D. Van Leeuwen
Creator of Summer Bridge Activities™✸

Ms. Hansen

TAKES YOU INSIDE

Summer Bridge Activities™ ❦

The exercises that are found in Summer Bridge Activities™ ❦ (SBA) are easy to understand and are presented in a way that allows your child to review familiar skills and then be progressively challenged on more difficult subjects. In addition to academic exercises, Summer Bridge Activities™ ❦ contains many other activities to reinforce reading comprehension, phonemic awareness, and word recognition.

Sections of Summer Bridge Activities™ ❦

 There are three sections to Summer Bridge Activities™ ❦; the first and second sections review, the third previews.

 Each section begins with an SBA Incentive Contract Calendar.

 Each day your child will complete an activity in reading, writing, arithmetic, and language skills. The activities progressively become more challenging.

 Each page is numbered by day.

 Your child will need a pencil, a ruler, an eraser, and crayons to complete the activities.

Books Children Love to Read

SBA contains a Summer Reading Book List with a variety of titles, including many that are found in the Accelerated Reader Program.

RBP recommends that parents read to their Pre–Kindergarten and Kindergarten–1st Grade children 5–10 minutes each day, and ask questions about the story to reinforce comprehension. For higher grade levels, RBP recommends the following daily reading times: Grades 1–2, 10–20 minutes; Grades 2–3, 20–30 minutes; Grades 3–4, 30–45 minutes; Grades 4–5 and 5–6, 45–60 minutes.

It is important that the parent and child decide an amount of reading time and write it on the SBA Incentive Contract Calendar.

SBA Incentive Contract Calendars

Calendars are located at the beginning of each section.

We suggest that the parent and child sign the SBA Incentive Contract Calendar before the child begins each section.

When your child completes one day of Summer Bridge Activities™ ❦, she may colour or initial the pencil.

Refer to the recommended reading times. When your child completes the agreed reading time each day, she may colour or initial the book.

The parent may initial the SBA Incentive Contract Calendar once the activities have been completed.

Let your child explore and experiment with the "Discover Something New" activities found on the back of each SBA Incentive Contract Calendar.

10 Helpful Hints on How to Maximize Summer Bridge Activities™

 1 First, let your child explore the book. Flip through the pages and look at the activities with your child to help him become familiar with the book.

2 Help select a good time for reading or working on the activities. Suggest a time before your child has played outside and becomes too tired to do her work.

 3 Provide any necessary materials. A pencil, a ruler, an eraser, and crayons are all that are required.

 4 Offer positive guidance. Children need a great deal of guidance. Remember, the activities are not meant to be tests. You want to create a relaxed and positive attitude toward learning. Work through at least one example on each page with your child. "Think aloud," and show your child how to solve problems.

 5 Give your child plenty of time to think. You may be surprised by how much children can do on their own.

 6 Stretch your child's thinking beyond the page. If you are reading a storybook, you might ask, "What do you think will happen next?" or "What would you do if this happened to you?" Encourage your child to name objects that begin with certain letters, or count the number of items in your shopping cart. Also, children often enjoy making up their own stories with illustrations.

 7 Reread stories and occasionally flip through completed pages. Completed pages and books will be a source of pride to your child and will help show how much he accomplished over the summer.

 8 Read and work on activities while outside. Take the workbook out in the backyard, to the park, or to a family camp out. It can be fun wherever you are!

9 Encourage siblings, babysitters, and neighbourhood children to help with reading and activities. Other children are often perfect for providing the one-on-one attention necessary to reinforce reading skills.

 10 Give plenty of approval! Stickers and stamps, or even a hand-drawn funny face are effective for recognizing a job well done. When your child completes the book, hang her Certificate of Completion where everyone can see it. At the end of the summer, your child can feel proud of her accomplishments and will be eager for school to start.

words to SOUND, READ, and W-r-i-t-e

At the end of each section are words to sound out, read, and spell.

Together you and your child can:

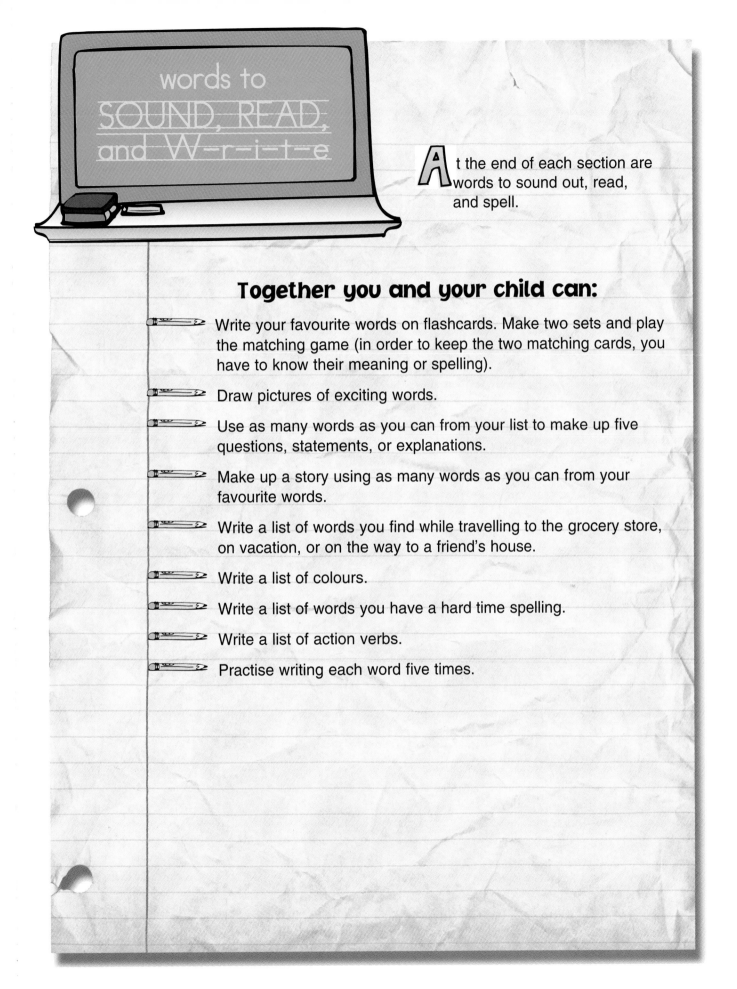

- Write your favourite words on flashcards. Make two sets and play the matching game (in order to keep the two matching cards, you have to know their meaning or spelling).

- Draw pictures of exciting words.

- Use as many words as you can from your list to make up five questions, statements, or explanations.

- Make up a story using as many words as you can from your favourite words.

- Write a list of words you find while travelling to the grocery store, on vacation, or on the way to a friend's house.

- Write a list of colours.

- Write a list of words you have a hard time spelling.

- Write a list of action verbs.

- Practise writing each word five times.

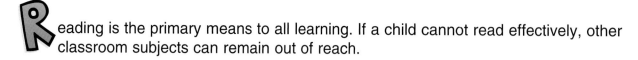

Reading is the primary means to all learning. If a child cannot read effectively, other classroom subjects can remain out of reach.

You were probably the first person to introduce your child to the wonderful world of reading. As your child grows, it is important to continue encouraging his interest in reading to support the skills being taught in school.

This summer, make reading a priority in your household. Set aside time each day to read aloud to your child at bedtime or after lunch or dinner. Encourage your child to take a break from playing, and stretch out with a book found on the Summer Bridge Activities™ ❀ Reading List. Choose a title that you have never read, or introduce your child to some of the books you enjoyed when you were that age! Books only seem to get better with time!

Visit the library to find books that meet your child's specific interests. Ask a librarian which books are popular among children of your child's grade. Take advantage of summer storytelling activities at the library. Ask the librarian about other resources, such as stories on cassette, compact disc, and the Internet.

Encourage reading in all settings and daily activities. Encourage your child to read house numbers, street signs, window banners, and packaging labels. Encourage your child to tell stories using pictures.

Best of all, show your child how much YOU like to read! Sit down with your child when she reads and enjoy a good book yourself. After dinner, share stories and ideas from newspapers and magazines that might interest your child. Make reading a way of life this summer!

Reading List

Try looking for favourites of your own from the list,
and share those with your child this summer.

By Author

Adler, David
*Cam Jansen and the Mystery of
the Dinosaur Bones*

Aliki
Digging Up Dinosaurs

Allard, Harry
Miss Nelson books

❋ **Atwood, Margaret**
Princess Prunella and the Purple Peanut

Barracca, Debra and Sal
The Adventures of Taxi Dog

❋ **Beck, Andrea**
Elliot Bakes a Cake
Elliot's Emergency

Berenstain, Stan & Jan
The Berenstain Bears books

Blocksma, Mary
Yoo Hoo, Moon!

Bond, Michael
A Bear Called Paddington

❋ **Bourgeois, Paulette**
Big Sarah's Little Boots
The Many Hats of Mr. Minches
Too Many Chickens

Brandenberg, Franz
Nice New Neighbors

Brenner, Barbara
Annie's Pet

❋ **Brownridge, William Roy**
The Final Game
The Moccasin Goalie

Brunhoff, Laurent De
Babar books

Byars, Betsy Cromer
Hooray for the Golly Sisters!
The Golly Sisters Go West

Chorao, Kay
Oink and Pearl

Christian, Mary Blount
Penrod's Picture

❋ **Cleaver, Elizabeth**
The Loon's Necklace

Coerr, Eleanor
Chang's Paper Pony

❋ **Downie, Mary Alice**
Jenny Greenteeth

Gackenbach, Dick
Mag the Magnificent
Hattie Rabbit

❋ **Garrett, Jennifer**
The Queen Who Stole the Sky

Gelman, Rita
More Spaghetti, I Say!

❋ **Green, John F.**
There's a Dragon in My Closet

Himmelman, John
The Super Camper Caper

Hutchins, Pat
Don't Forget the Bacon!

Kessler, Ethel and Leonard
Stan the Hot Dog Man

❋ **Kovalski, Maryann**
Frank and Zelda
Take Me Out to the Ball Game
Wheels on the Bus

❋ **Little, Jean**
Jess Was the Brave One
Once upon a Golden Apple

Martchenko, Michael
Birdfeeder Banquet

Mayer, Mercer
Just Me books

McCully, Emily Arnold
Zaza's Big Break

McDermott, Gerald
The Stonecutter: A Japanese Folk Tale

Miles, Miska
Annie and the Old One

Mozelle, Shirley
Zack's Alligator

Morgan, Allen
Andrew and the Wild Bikes
Brendon and the Wolves
Matthew and the Midnight books
Sadie and the Snowman
Sam and the Tigers

O'Connor, Jane
Super Cluck
The Teeny Tiny Woman

Pickett, Anola
Old Enough for Magic

Pinkwater, Daniel Manus
I Was a Second Grade Werewolf

Porte, Barbara Ann
Harry's Visit

Poulin, Stephane
Animals in Winter
Benjamin and the Pillow Saga
Can You Catch Josephine?
Could You Stop Josephine?
Have You Seen Josephine?

Rey, H.A.
The *Curious George* series

Reynolds, Marilyn
A Dog for a Friend
The New Land a First Year on the Prairie

Richards, Nancy Wilcox
Farmer Joe Goes to the City
Farmer Joe's Hot Day

Schwartz, Alvin
There Is a Carrot in My Ear and Other Noodle Tales

Sharmat, Mitchell
Gregory, the Terrible Eater

Sharmat, Marjorie Weinman
A Big Fat Enormous Lie

Skelton, Mora
The Baritone Cat

Small, David
Imogene's Antlers

Staunton, Ted
Miss Fishley Afloat
Puddleman

Steig, William
The Zabajaba Jungle

Stinson, Kathy
Red Is Best
Teddy Rabbit

Taylor, C. J.
How Two-Feather Was Saved from Loneliness

The Funny Side Up Books
Dinosaur Jokes

Thurman, Mark
One Too Many

Titus, Eve
Anatole books

Voigt, Cynthia
Stories about Rosie

Waber, Bernard
Bernard

Watterton, Betty
Plain Noodles
A Salmon for Simon

Wynne-Jones, Tim
Architect of the Moon
I'll Make You Small
The Last Piece of Sky
Zoom Away
Zoom at Sea

Yolen, Jane
Sleeping Ugly

Zimmermann, Werner
Snow Day
Twelve Months Make a Year

SBA Incentive Contract

calendar

for the month of:

My Incentive Is:

Child's Signature

Parent's Signature

When you have completed a daily activity, colour a

Day 1
Day 2
Day 3
Day 4
Day 5
Day 6
Day 7

Day 8
Day 9
Day 10
Day 11
Day 12
Day 13
Day 14
Day 15

When you have completed [ ] minutes of reading, colour a

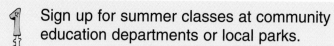

1 Sign up for summer classes at community education departments or local parks.

2 Make a chart for summer chores with incentives.

3 Write to a relative about your summer plans.

4 Check the library for free children's programs.

5 Boost reading—make labels for household objects.

6 Start a journal of summer fun.

Fun Activity Ideas to Go Along with the First Section!

7 Zoo contest—find the most African animals.

8 Shop together—use a calculator to compare prices per kilogram.

9 Tune up those bikes. Wash them, too.

10 Arrange photo albums.

11 Play flashlight tag.

12 Check out a science book—try some experiments.

13 Make up a story at dinner. Each person adds a new paragraph.

14 Learn about the summer solstice. Time the sunrise and the sunset.

15 Bubble fun: 78.8 ml of liquid dishwashing soap, plus 1.9 litres of water. Use cans or pipe cleaners for dippers.

Mathematics—Numeration

Write to 200.

101	102		104				108		110
111				115				119	
	122								130
						137			
141									150
		153							
				165					
									180
					186				
191								198	

Word Study—Contractions

Write the two words found in each contraction.

EXAMPLE:

1. can't   <u>cannot</u>
2. we're   _____
3. I've   _____
4. it's   _____
5. we'll   _____
6. you've   _____
7. I'd   _____
8. isn't   _____

9. didn't   _____
10. aren't   _____
11. you're   _____
12. I'll   _____
13. she's   _____
14. won't   _____
15. I'm   _____
16. let's   _____

Word Study—Synonyms

Write a synonym from the Word Bank that has almost the same meaning as the underlined word in the sentence.

EXAMPLE:
1. Here comes the <u>furry</u> cat. **fuzzy**

Word Bank

like
fuzzy
silly
largest
watch
turn
yell
leaped
unhappy
scared

2. He <u>jumped</u> out of the car. _____

3. Let's clap and <u>shout</u> for our team. _____

4. I <u>enjoy</u> watching ball games. _____

5. Were the children <u>frightened</u>? _____

6. The <u>sad</u> man was crying. _____

7. Did you <u>see</u> the frog jump? _____

8. He is riding the <u>biggest</u> horse. _____

9. Watch the top <u>spin</u> around. _____

10. Did you see that <u>funny</u> movie? _____

Language—Capitalization

Colour the spaces yellow if the names are capitalized correctly. Colour the other spaces blue.

Bob jones
Keith grams
Julie Hodd
Kim Sue
Sandy Hopps
Don brown
Nikki King
Ann noble
Scott Green
Jill fox
don Smith
Wendy Morse
jane Doe
Tom Young
Sam chee
Pam Gold
Pat Fisher
Mike miller
Mary Waters
joe Peters

Mathematics—Addition and Subtraction Review

Add or subtract.

7	0	8	6	9	9	7	4
+ 2	+ 3	+ 3	+ 2	+ 0	+ 1	+ 3	+ 3

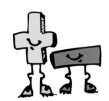

3	5	5	10	7	6	9	8
− 2	− 0	− 2	− 2	− 3	− 4	− 5	− 0

5	6	7	8	2	5	10	9
− 3	+ 4	− 2	− 4	+ 2	+ 5	− 5	− 8

Phonics—Reviewing Blends

Fill in the missing blends.

| fl, | pl, | bl, | spr, | sl, | sk, | sn, | st, | dr, | br, | pr, | fr, | pl, | gr, | cr |

1. The red and blue ____owers we ____anted will ____oom in the
   ____ing.

2. The boys and girls like to go ____edding and ice ____ating when
   it ____ows.

3. That ____ory is about a ____agon who ____eathed fire and a
   princess who kissed a ____og, then turned him into a ____ince.

4. My yellow, pur____e and ____een ____ayons ____oke when I
   ____opped them on the ____oor.

Reading Comprehension—Sequencing Events

Read the story. Number the events in the order that they happened.

The Alarm Clock

Rob was sleeping when his alarm clock started ringing. He jumped up, made his bed, and washed his face. Rob put on his clothes and started down the stairs to go eat breakfast. When he passed the window in the hall, he saw that it was still night. "Oh, no," he said, "my alarm clock went off at the wrong time!" Rob went back to his bedroom and got back in bed.

☐ Rob went back to bed.

☐ Rob's alarm clock rang.

☐ Rob saw that it was still night.

☐ Rob made his bed and washed his face.

☐ Rob started down to breakfast.

Reading Comprehension—Classifying Words

Read the words below. Choose a word from the word box that describes each group of words below. Write the word on the blank.

tools	weather	flavours	vegetables	fruits
animals	drinks	months	numbers	

cow, horse, goat	chocolate, strawberry, vanilla	one, nine, twenty
_____	_____	_____
rain, snow, sun	February, July, October	milk, juice, soda pop
_____	_____	_____
saw, hammer, drill	pear, banana, apple	carrots, corn, celery
_____	_____	_____

Mathematics—Reviewing Time

Write the correct time on the small clocks and draw hands on the big clocks.

12:00

_____:_____

9:30

_____:_____

6:00

_____:_____

Word Study—Understanding Words with Suffixes

Match each group of words to the word with the same meaning.

EXAMPLE:

1. very cheery   helpful

2. couldn't sleep   thankful

3. many colours   cheerful

4. without sun   colourful

5. helps a lot   sleepless

6. a lot of thanks   sunless

The words in these sentences are mixed up. Write them correctly. Do not forget to add capital letters and the correct ending punctuation mark: (.) or (?).

1. birds do live where

   _____

2. very my hard works dad

   _____

3. swim can like fish a i

   _____

4. green grass the is

   _____

5. water do fish in live

   _____

6. ate lunch for Grayson pizza

   _____

Word Study—Identifying Correctly Spelled Words

Colour in the circle next to the correct spelling for each word.

EXAMPLE:

1. ● a. what   ○ b. wat   ○ c. whut

2. ○ a. whare   ○ b. where   ○ c. whar

3. ○ a. when   ○ b. wen   ○ c. whene

4. ○ a. wiye   ○ b. wye   ○ c. why

Mathematics—Problem Solving

Answer the question: How many are there in all? Write the problem.

EXAMPLE:

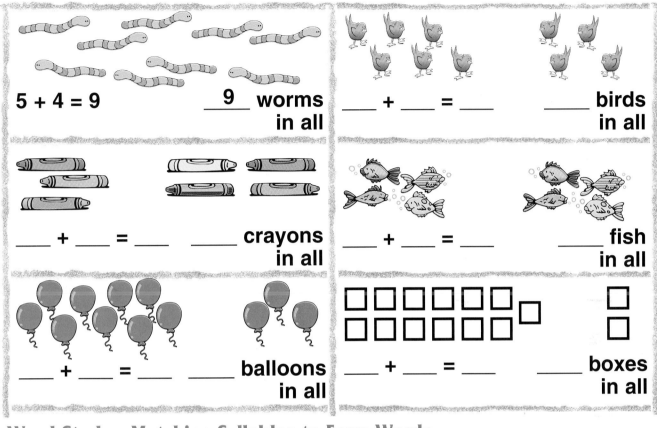

5 + 4 = 9   ___9___ worms in all

___ + ___ = ___   _____ birds in all

___ + ___ = ___   _____ crayons in all

___ + ___ = ___   _____ fish in all

___ + ___ = ___   _____ balloons in all

___ + ___ = ___   _____ boxes in all

Word Study—Matching Syllables to Form Words

Finish the words by drawing a line to the correct ending. Write the words.

EXAMPLE:

spi	key	_____
cray	der	_____
wag	der	_____
tur	on	_____
mon	key	_____
thun	on	_____
don	der	_____
lad	key	_____
drag	on	_____
won	der	_____

Reading—Using Context Clues

Write the correct word on the blank to complete each sentence.

1. Cats are _____ animals.
   freely   friendly   friend

2. I'd _____ help you feed your cat.
   gladly   highly   gladder

3. Matt called _____ for his cat.
   loud   loudly   tightly

4. Cats like to _____.
   playing   play   clay

5. My friend's cat _____ all day.
   sleeps   sleeping   beeps

Word Study—Identifying and Classifying Singular and Plural Words

Words can be *singular* (one) or *plural* (more than one). Use both forms of the word and label them correctly.

EXAMPLE:

a.	birds	**more**	**bird**	**one**
b.	girl	**one**	**girls**	**more**
1.	trees	**more**	_____	_____
2.	boxes	_____	_____	_____
3.	wheel	**one**	**wheels**	_____
4.	ape	_____	_____	_____
5.	shoes	_____	**shoe**	**one**
6.	peach	_____	_____	_____
7.	shirt	_____	_____	_____
8.	nickels	**more**	**nickel**	_____
9.	plum	_____	_____	_____
10.	pencils	_____	_____	-

Mathematics—Recognizing Amounts of Money

Circle the coins that equal the amount of money shown.

34¢ =

72¢ =

25¢ =

49¢ =

18¢ =

Language—Identifying and Classifying Nouns and Verbs

Find your way though the maze by colouring all of the naming words (*nouns*) green. Colour all of the action words (*verbs*) yellow. Colour all of the other words orange.

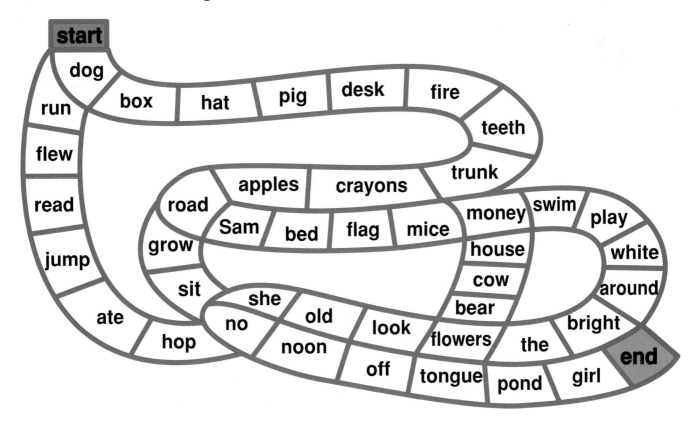

Language—Punctuation Review

Here is a silly story. Put a (.), (?), or (!) at the end of each sentence. Make the first letter of each sentence uppercase. Then, draw a picture of this "silly thing" the way that you imagine it looks.

i saw a very silly thing it had a very funny shape it did not make any noise it had spots that changed colour and big feet with green toes it had little hands and a big, fat, pink nose i hope it doesn't hurt me maybe it will be nice we might become friends and play i wonder what it likes to eat i hope it's not me

Word Study—Identifying Pairs of Synonyms

Match each pair of synonyms, and then, circle them in the puzzle.

Word List

EXAMPLE:

quick	start
begin	rot
choose	ill
error	fast
decay	join
sick	silly
easy	remain
connect	select
stay	mistake
foolish	simple

```
a b c z o w r y m p d e f h j k m o s i c
e a s y a d f l d e c a y r b m b d k r o
o p s q u i c k q r s r t u e v w x y z n
b z i o e v f u v w x o z e g d f k l k n
c d m n o p a a p y t t o u i k l a c b e
d k p w x z s y p q x a u t n s t a r t c
o u l o o i t a d f f e s e l e c t o e t
z a e m n o p q r s o t u v r w x c y z j
k i e r r o r s t u o p k d e b a h i u o
l o m i s t a k e z l u p i m g h o k o i
m u g j l p q g r s i v w u a z g o i l n
i p b d f g l i o z s s p o i u i s g o m
l z w x y z u g a b h d l e n i u e o b c
l s i c k p s i l l y m u s t a y y i o e
```

Mathematics—Single Column Addition

Remember to add all three numerals.

2	4	5	9	7	4	5	3
3	4	1	1	2	0	5	3
+2	+2	+1	+0	+1	+4	+2	+3

6	8	1	5	6	2	3	5
0	1	2	2	1	5	7	5
+2	+2	+6	+5	+7	+4	+1	+5

2 + 2 + 2 = _____   0 + 0 + 8 = _____   1 + 0 + 8 = _____

5 + 1 + 1 = _____   2 + 5 + 3 = _____   9 + 2 + 2 = _____

3 + 2 + 3 = _____   2 + 3 + 4 = _____   4 + 5 + 1 = _____

Word Study—Identifying When to Add "d" or "ed"

When we add -ed or -d to a word, it shows something was done before.
We use -d when the word ends in a vowel, and -ed when the word ends in a
consonant. Look at the word, say the word, add -ed or -d to the word, and
say the word again.

EXAMPLE:

wipe__**d**____   clean_____   rain_____   bake_____

cook_____   walk_____   play_____   paint_____

watch_____   work_____   talk_____   dress_____

bath_____   wait_____   time_____   work_____

Word Study—Identifying and Dividing Compound Words

Read the sentence, underline the compound word, and then, draw a line between the two words.

EXAMPLE:

1. Mary Ann lives on a <u>house|boat</u>.
2. My father won the downhill race.
3. A raindrop hit the white bunny on the nose.
4. Do you understand how to do this?
5. The fireplace was very dirty.
6. Did someone ring your doorbell at 3 A.M.?
7. Pigs, horses, and cows are in the barnyard.
8. I had to clean my bedroom this morning.
9. The snowflakes fell very thick and heavy this winter.
10. My friends and I went downstairs to see a video.
11. I ate both drumsticks for my lunch.

Reading—Classifying Groups of Words

Write the words in the correct ball.

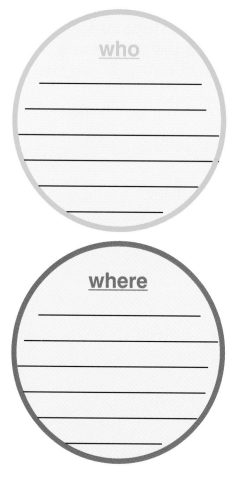

who

where

big truck
7:00 p.m.
in a box
outside
Aunt Marge
noon
last month
Tom
under a tree
in my bed
tomorrow
Grandpa
jet
baby
book
hot dog

EXAMPLE:

what
big truck

when

Write how many tens and ones. Then, write the total.

EXAMPLE:

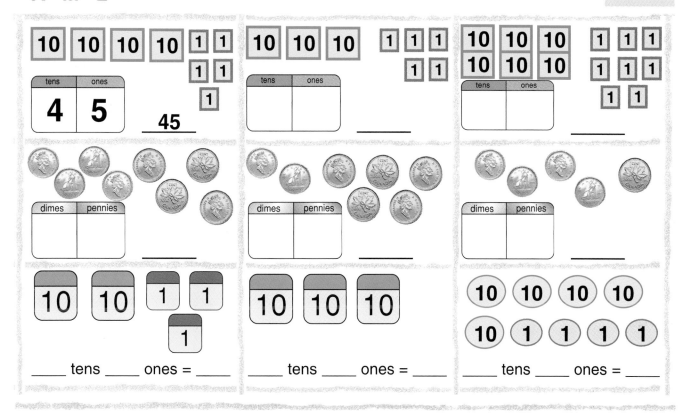

	tens	ones
	4	5	45

_____ tens _____ ones = _____

_____ tens _____ ones = _____

_____ tens _____ ones = _____

Language—Completing a Story Starter

Finish the story. Give it a title, and draw a picture for it.

_____

My friend, _____, and I
went for a hike in the mountains. At a
steep place on the path, we slipped
and fell into a hole. We went down
and down. We didn't think we would
ever stop falling. When we hit the
bottom of the hole, we found . . .

_____

_____

_____

_____

Reading—Finding the Main Idea

Circle the main idea of the stories.

I love books. In the summer I go to the library every other day. I check out books about horses and airplanes. I also like to read about football. I do not like

how quiet I have to be in the library.

a. football books

b. at the library

c. being quiet

Sometimes, we have dreams that frighten us. Once, I dreamed I was falling over a cliff. I woke up shaking, I was so scared. My friend, Nan, dreamed a monster was coming after her. She hid in a

big box so he could not find her. She woke up just as the monster put his hand in the box.

a. falling over a cliff

b. dreaming of monsters

c. scary dreams

Reading—Answering Questions; Noting Detail

Put an X on the line to answer each question.

1. Which sentence names three things?
    ___ Allie took a book, a bag, and an umbrella to school.
    ___ Allie took a bookbag and an umbrella to school.

2. Which sentence names four people?
    ___ Grayson, Mary Jane, and I went shopping.
    ___ Grayson, Mary, Jane, and I went shopping.

3. Which sentence names two things?
    ___ Tanner put the lunch, box, and book on the table.
    ___ Tanner put the lunchbox and the book on the table.

Mathematics—Classifying Numerals Using Symbols

Greater than is > , and less than is < . Put the correct sign in each circle.

2 ◯ 4   19 ◯ 91   14 ◯ 4

9 ◯ 10   64 ◯ 46   29 ◯ 30

16 ◯ 20   32 ◯ 23   71 ◯ 18

124 ◯ 216   592 ◯ 324   2 + 4 ◯ 1 + 4   5 + 4 ◯ 8 − 2

322 ◯ 100   985 ◯ 850   9 − 2 ◯ 6 + 2   3 − 2 ◯ 5 − 2

648 ◯ 846   745 ◯ 746   4 + 4 ◯ 1 + 4   7 − 3 ◯ 1 + 2

Reading—Using Context Clues

Read each sentence. Choose one of the two words in the box to complete the sentence. Write the word on the blank.

1. Have you seen my _____?

2. Let's go to the _____ and catch some fish.

3. Tanner rides the _____ to school.

4. Denise is growing corn in her _____.

5. Miss Hansen is our _____.

6. Matt _____ when he hit his finger with the hammer.

7. Rob went to camp with his _____.

8. Lori lost one of her _____.

park	pants
lock	lake
bus	brass
guard	garden
teacher	teach
yellow	yelled
bother	brother
slippers	skippers

Reading—Making Inferences

Read the stories. Circle the words that tell what happens next.

1.

Matt put his arms around the box. He could not lift it. He would need some help. The box was too heavy for him.

Matt will_____.

a. run outside and play
b. go ask his dad for help
c. hit the box with an ax
d. send the box to his friend

2.

The children were playing outside. It started to get dark. They could see a flash of light and hear a loud sound. The wind began to blow.

"Let's go," shouted Ann. "It's _____."

a. time to eat
b. going to blow us away
c. going to rain soon
d. time for bed

3.

Mary likes to ride her bike to school. One day she rode her bike over some glass.

The next day Mary walked to school because_____.

a. she liked to walk
b. her bike had a flat tire
c. her brother rode her bike
d. her bike was red

Language—Brainstorming Descriptive Words

**Design and colour your own T-shirt.
Write at least 10 words to describe it.**

_____
_____
_____
_____
_____
_____
_____
_____

Mathematics—Subtraction Review
Subtract.

6	3	10	7	9	6	9	10
− 4	− 1	− 8	− 5	− 2	− 6	− 8	− 2

4 − 2 = _____   10 − 5 = _____   7 − 3 = _____

3 − 0 = _____   9 − 4 = _____   8 − 5 = _____

7 − 4 = _____   8 − 4 = _____   10 − 6 = _____

11	12	10	13	9	14	11	13
− 2	− 4	− 0	− 5	− 7	− 8	− 5	− 9

Word Study—Adding the Suffix "ing" to Words

When we add -ing to a word, it shows that something is being done now.
Look at the word, say the word, add -ing to the word, and say the word again.

go**ing**_____   say_____   do_____   tell_____

sleep_____   walk_____   read_____   sew_____

paint_____   work_____   eat_____   drink_____

spell_____   cook_____   watch_____   talk_____

Reading—Answering General Questions with Sentences

Answer the questions. Write in complete sentences.

1. What do you use your ears for?

   _____

2. What do zoo workers do for the animals?

   _____

3. What would you use to make a cage for a hamster?

   _____

4. What are dogs, cats, cows, and deer?

   _____

5. How did you get to and from school last year?

   _____

6. How old is your best friend?

   _____

Reading—Following Directions; Classifying Words

Read and follow the directions carefully.

1. Make a box around all of the animals.
2. Put a circle around all of the tools.
3. Draw a line under all of the things we wear.
4. Put a ⭐ on all of the places in a house.
5. Write an **X** on all of the noises.

crash	saw	hammer	bedroom
playroom	bang	kitchen	bear
yell	pants	fox	bathroom
whisper	rabbit	wrench	boom
closet	shoes	elephant	hat
shirt	hall	deer	den

Mathematics—Subtraction

Subtract 6

8

12

9

11

7

13

Subtract 8

8

11

12

19

10

14

Subtract 7

14

8

7

10

12

9

Geography—Using a Mapping Key to Locate Information

Look at the map and map key to answer the questions.

1. How many stores are there?

_____

2. What street has the most houses?

_____

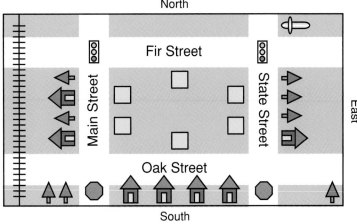

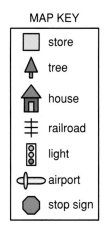

3. What two streets does the railroad go across?
_____ and _____

4. How many trees are west of the airport? _____

5. What two streets have stop signs? _____ and _____

6. What three streets have traffic lights?
_____ , _____ , and _____

Reading—Using Words Ending with "ion" in Sentences

Fill in the blanks. Use the words from the box.

1. This orange has ten _____ in it.
2. A car is one kind of _____.
3. Can you answer my _____?
4. We went on a _____ to Hawaii.
5. My brother and I have a stamp _____.
6. I like to do hard _____ problems.
7. The train stops at every _____.
8. We needed some _____ from the wind.
9. Is Japan a big _____?
10. Linda put some _____ on her hands.
11. Is one-half a _____?
12. Do not _____ this secret to Donald.

| vacation |
| station |
| sections |
| nation |
| addition |
| mention |
| collection |
| lotion |
| transportation |
| fraction |
| question |
| protection |

Reading—Using Number Words

Fill in the boxes with number words. Use some words more than once.

EXAMPLE:

1. Tanner wakes up at **s** **e** **v** **e** **n** o'clock.

2. He eats breakfast at [ ][ ][ ][ ] o'clock.

3. Tanner catches thebus at [ ][ ][ ][ ][ ] thirty.

4. School starts at [ ][ ][ ][ ] o'clock.

5. Recess is at [ ][ ][ ] o'clock in the morning and [ ][ ][ ]

   o'clock in the afternoon.

6. Tanner eats lunch at [ ][ ][ ][ ][ ][ ] o'clock.

7. School is out at [ ][ ][ ][ ][ ] thirty.

8. Tanner eats dinner at [ ][ ][ ][ ][ ] o'clock.

9. He plays until bedtime at [ ][ ][ ][ ][ ] o'clock.

Mathematics—Identifying Number Words

Write the numeral on the line beside each number word.

forty	_____	eight	_____	one	_____
sixteen	_____	seventeen	_____	eighteen	_____
four	_____	fifty	_____	thirty	_____
nine	_____	two	_____	ninety-nine	_____
twelve	_____	nineteen	_____	seven	_____
ten	_____	eleven	_____	thirteen	_____
fifteen	_____	thirty-three	_____	fourteen	_____
twenty	_____	five	_____	six	_____

Word Study—Rhyming Words

Write five words that rhyme with each key word.

EXAMPLE:

sack
back
_____
_____
_____
_____

rock
_____
_____
_____
_____
_____

deck
_____
_____
_____
_____
_____

lick
_____
_____
_____
_____
_____

truck
_____
_____
_____
_____
_____

queen
_____
_____
_____
_____
_____

king
_____
_____
_____
_____
_____

song
_____
_____
_____
_____
_____

rung
_____
_____
_____
_____
_____

jump
_____
_____
_____
_____
_____

Language—Recognizing the Meaning of Pronouns

Write what or who the underlined words mean.

EXAMPLE: The boys ran away. <u>They</u> ran to school.

They = **boys**

1. Carla and I like horses. We ride <u>them</u> every day.
   them = _____
2. Grandma called today. <u>She</u> is coming to see us.
   She = _____
3. Joe would like to fly in a jet. <u>He</u> has never been in <u>one</u>.
   He = _____ one = _____
4. This summer, I am at camp. I like it <u>here</u>.
   here = _____
5. I lost my best umbrella. <u>It</u> is blue.
   It = _____
6. Lee has two dogs. <u>They</u> are both black.
   They = _____
7. Ted and I are late for the movie. John is waiting for <u>us</u>.
   us = _____
8. I left a note for Mom. <u>It</u> tells <u>her</u> where I am.
   It = _____ her = _____

Word Study—Identifying Correctly Spelled Words

Read each sentence. Look carefully at the underlined word. Is it spelled right or wrong? Mark your answer.

EXAMPLE: | | **Right** | **Wrong** |
|---|---|---|
| 1. Randy <u>ate</u> toast with jam on it. | ● | ○ |
| 2. We <u>wunt</u> to the store for some candy. | ○ | ○ |
| 3. The dog will <u>hund</u> for his bone. | ○ | ○ |
| 4. We will <u>plant</u> our garden tonight. | ○ | ○ |
| 5. The <u>keng</u> asked the queen to come quick. | ○ | ○ |
| 6. This is the <u>ent</u> of my story. | ○ | ○ |
| 7. I want my hair to grow very <u>long</u>. | ○ | ○ |
| 8. <u>Think</u> of a good name for a pet. | ○ | ○ |
| 9. Do you like to <u>sing</u> with friends? | ○ | ○ |
| 10. Do not let the cat <u>lant</u> on my bed. | ○ | ○ |

Mathematics—Place Value

What does the circled digit mean? Circle the answer. Be sure to read the words.

EXAMPLE:

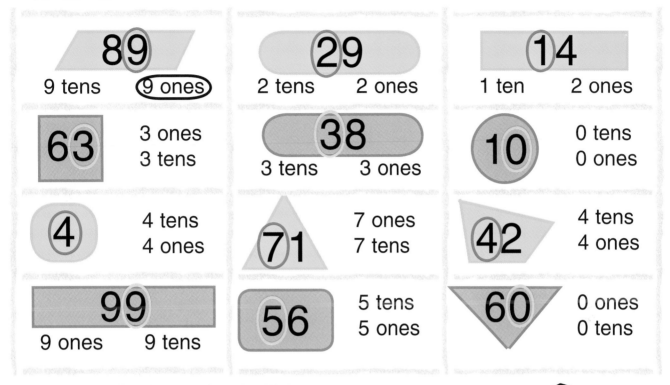

89   9 tens   (9 ones)

29   2 tens   2 ones

(14)   1 ten   2 ones

63   3 ones / 3 tens

38   3 tens   3 ones

10   0 tens / 0 ones

4   4 tens / 4 ones

71   7 ones / 7 tens

42   4 tens / 4 ones

99   9 ones   9 tens

56   5 tens / 5 ones

60   0 ones / 0 tens

Language—Capitalization in Titles

Rule: The first and all other important words in a story or a book title begin with an uppercase letter. Write these story titles correctly.

EXAMPLE:

1. an exciting camping trip _____**An Exciting Camping Trip**_____

2. my ride on an elephant _____

3. the day we missed school _____

4. pets are fun _____

5. a real fire drill _____

6. my vacation this summer _____

7. a lost puppy _____

8. walking in the rain _____

Mathematics—Graphing: Interpretations

Study the pictograph. Read the questions and circle your answer.

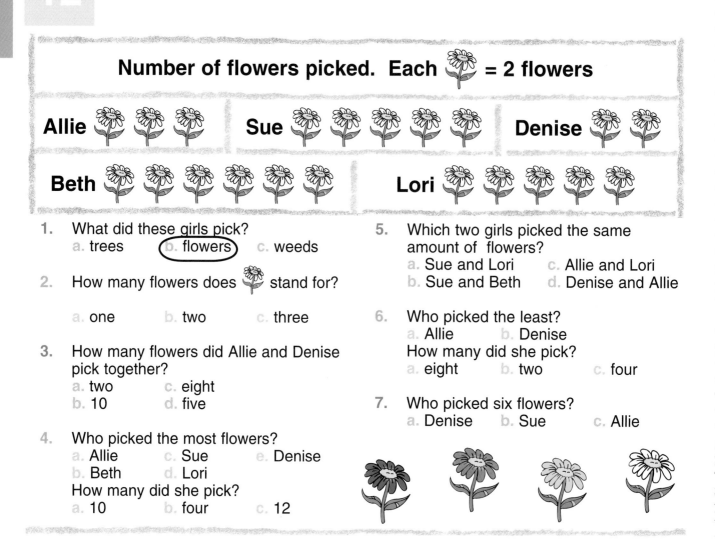

Number of flowers picked. Each 🌼 = 2 flowers

Allie 🌼 🌼 🌼

Sue 🌼 🌼 🌼 🌼 🌼

Denise 🌼 🌼

Beth 🌼 🌼 🌼 🌼 🌼 🌼

Lori 🌼 🌼 🌼 🌼 🌼

1. What did these girls pick?
   a. trees   (b. flowers)   c. weeds

2. How many flowers does 🌼 stand for?

   a. one   b. two   c. three

3. How many flowers did Allie and Denise pick together?
   a. two   c. eight
   b. 10   d. five

4. Who picked the most flowers?
   a. Allie   c. Sue   e. Denise
   b. Beth   d. Lori
   How many did she pick?
   a. 10   b. four   c. 12

5. Which two girls picked the same amount of flowers?
   a. Sue and Lori   c. Allie and Lori
   b. Sue and Beth   d. Denise and Allie

6. Who picked the least?
   a. Allie   b. Denise
   How many did she pick?
   a. eight   b. two   c. four

7. Who picked six flowers?
   a. Denise   b. Sue   c. Allie

Language—Creative Writing

Write a dinner menu for a dragon. Draw a picture to go with it.

Dragon Dinner Menu

Read the story. Write the problem and the answer.

1. Tanner had 8 balls. He lost 2 of them. How many balls does he have now?

   EXAMPLE:

   __8 – 2__ = __6__ balls

2. Allie has 4 dolls. She got 6 more for her birthday. How many dolls does Allie have?

   _____ = _____ dolls

3. We had 11 goldfish. Our cat ate 9 of them. How many goldfish were not eaten?

   _____ = _____ goldfish

4. Rob walked 3 kilometres, Lori walked 6 kilometres, and Matt walked 4 kilometres. How many kilometres did the children walk in all?

   _____ = _____ kilometres

5. Matt has two dogs, Tina and Joy. Tina had 8 puppies and Joy had 4. How many puppies are there in all?

   _____ = _____ puppies

6. I bought one dozen eggs (12). On the way home from the store, I broke 5 of them. How many eggs did not get broken?

   _____ = _____ eggs

Word Study—Identifying Singular and Plural Words

Circle and write the correct word for each sentence. Remember: When you add "-s" or "-es" to a word, it means more than one.

1. Two _____ went for a ride.   **girl   girls**
2. My _____ broke when it fell.   **dish   dishes**
3. Which _____ is yours?   **pencil   pencils**
4. Put all of the _____ back on the shelf.   **book   books**
5. Martin carried the _____ in a basket.   **potato   potatoes**
6. How many _____ were in the race?   **boat   boats**
7. May I have a piece of _____?   **pie   pies**
8. Where are my _____?   **shoe   shoes**
9. There are two _____ on my street.   **house   houses**
10. I have a lot of nice _____.   **friend   friends**

Reading—Identifying Word Meanings

What does the underlined word mean? Circle your answer.

1. She has on a <u>dark</u> green dress.
   a. not light   b. night

2. We were <u>safe</u> on the rock.
   a. without danger   b. place to keep things

3. Sam had to be home before <u>dark</u>.
   a. night   b. morning   c. day

4. Can you <u>lift</u> this box?
   a. pick up   b. put down   c. turn over

5. I need <u>several</u> people to help me.
   a. none   b. one   c. some   d. hundreds

6. My clothes were still <u>damp</u>.
   a. dry   b. front   c. wet   d. pretty

Word Study—Using Triple Blends to Make Words

Fill in the banks with *str-*, *spr-*, *spl-*, or *thr-*, and then, follow the directions at the bottom of the page.

___ ___ ___ ead	___ ___ ___ eet	___ ___ ___ ang
___ ___ ___ it	___ ___ ___ ong	___ ___ ___ ay
___ ___ ___ ough	___ ___ ___ ash	___ ___ ___ ow
___ ___ ___ ee	___ ___ ___ ing	___ ___ ___ atter

1. Colour the **spr-** words yellow.
2. Put an **X** on the **spl-** words.
3. Circle the **thr-** words.
4. Colour the **str-** words orange.

Mathematics—Identifying and Placing Signs Correctly

Write the missing signs (+, -, or =) in the circle.

6 ◯ 3 = 9	12 ◯ 6 = 6	4 ◯ 2 = 2	5 ◯ 2 = 3
4 + 3 ◯ 7	14 ◯ 1 = 15	12 ◯ 2 = 10	9 ◯ 5 = 4
9 ◯ 3 = 6	14 ◯ 4 = 10	14 − 7 ◯ 7	8 − 4 ◯ 4
4 ◯ 1 = 3	7 − 3 ◯ 4	3 ◯ 3 = 6	12 ◯ 2 = 14
8 ◯ 4 = 12	9 ◯ 2 = 11	11 ◯ 2 = 9	6 ◯ 7 = 13
7 + 3 ◯ 10	10 ◯ 3 = 13	12 − 4 ◯ 8	13 − 3 ◯ 10
10 ◯ 8 = 2	3 ◯ 8 = 11	10 + 2 ◯ 12	14 ◯ 1 = 15
4 ◯ 4 = 8	6 + 4 ◯ 10	0 + 9 ◯ 9	12 − 1 ◯ 11

Word Study—Adding Suffixes to Base Words

Look at each base word, and add the endings *-er* and *-est*.

thin   _____thinner_____   _____thinnest_____

slim   _____   _____

big   _____   _____

hot   _____   _____

red   _____   _____

Write the correct ending on each base word in the sentence.

1. That is the big_____ cake on the table.

2. My cheeks are red_____ than your coat.

3. Jenna is slim_____ than her brother.

4. Today is the hot_____ day we have had so far.

5. My sandwich is thin_____ than yours.

6. You need to make this cookie flat_____ than this.

Reading—Context Clues

Fill in the blanks. Use the words under the sentences.

1. We dressed in special _____ for the party.

   cloth   **clothes**   **clothed**

2. She turned on the _____ as we came in the room.

   light   **lighted**   **lighting**

3. We take our _____ when we go camping.

   lately   **tent**   **rain**

4. We had _____ for dinner.

   banks   **beaned**   **beans**

5. My bedroom is _____.

   blow   **blew**   **blue**

6. Ted _____, but he still missed the bus.

   hurried   **hundred**   **hopped**

Motor Skills—Practising Printing or Writing Skills

Asking questions may give us directions or information. Write or print these question-sentences.

1. Does this road go past our house?

2. What time is it now?

3. Can you show me the way to go?

4. How do you play this game?

5. Can you help me swim?

Mathematics—Numeration Order

Write the missing numbers.

| 300 | | 302 | | | 305 | | | 309 |

| | 311 | | | | | 316 | | | |

| 489 | | 491 | | | 495 | | |

| | 202 | | | | | | | 210 |

| 595 | | 597 | | | 601 | | |

Language—Capitalization and Punctuation

Circle the words that should have an uppercase letter. Put a period or a question mark at the end of each sentence.

EXAMPLE:

1. (rachel) lives in (quebec) (city) •
2. i live in fredricton, new brunswick____
3. where do you live____
4. mr. brown is my best neighbour____
5. was easter in april this year____
6. my mother shops at smith's market____
7. where is calgary, alberta____
8. look at what i have got____
9. children say "trick or treat" on hallowe'en____
10. do you like christmas or thanksgiving better____

Reading—Context Clues

Fill in the blanks. Use the words in the box.

trade	summer	cowboy	brought
circle	dry	ambulance	rust

1. The shovel had _____ all over it.
2. We stood in a _____ to play the game.
3. Do you like to go swimming in the _____?
4. My little brother wants to be a _____ when he grows up.
5. The _____ made a loud noise as it passed us.
6. I will _____ my banana for your orange.
7. Sammy _____ a big snake to school in a box.
8. The ground has not been _____ this summer.

Reading—Recognizing Sentences

Cross out each letter Z in the sentences. Read what the revealed sentences say.

1. Thezfarmerzhadzazlargezherdzofzcowszonzhiszfarm.
2. Peoplezlikeztozeatzcornzonzthezcob.
3. Howzoldzdozthezfarmer'szcowszget?
4. Myzunclezhaszhorseszonzhiszfarm.
5. Chickens,zducks,zpigs,zandzdogszalsozlive zonzfarms.

   Inzthiszbox,zdrawzazpicturezofzall zthezanimalszmentionedzinzthe zabovezsentences.

Words to Sound, Read, and Spell

able	boat	clean	door
about	body	clear	down
above	both	climb	draw
across	bottom	close	dress
act	bought	cloud	drew
add	bowl	coat	drink
afraid	break	cold	drive
after	bright	colour	drop
again	bring	come	drove
against	broke	complete	dry
ago	brother	cook	dump
air	brought	cool	during
all	build	copy	each
alphabet	bundle	corn	early
already	bury	corner	Earth
also	business	correct	east
always	busy	could	easy
among	buy	count	edge
angry	cabin	country	effect
animal	cage	course	eight
answer	came	cover	either
area	candle	cross	else
around	canyon	crowd	empty
back	captain	dance	enemy
ball	care	dark	engine
balm	carry	daughter	enjoy
basket	castle	decide	enough
bear	catch	deep	enter
beautiful	caught	different	even
because	cause	dinner	evening
before	center	dinosaur	ever
began	certain	direction	every
behind	change	disappear	exactly
believe	chick	distance	example
below	children	doctor	excite
between	choose	does	excuse
better	circle	dollar	expect
blow	city	done	explain
board	class	don't	extra

Words to Sound, Read, and Spell

eye	flour	hair	interest
face	flower	hand	invitation
fact	fly	happen	invite
faint	fold	happy	island
fair	follow	hard	jar
fall	food	have	job
family	foot	head	join
far	forest	hear	jump
farm	forget	heard	just
fast	found	heart	keep
father	four	heavy	kept
favourite	free	held	key
feed	fresh	help	kick
feel	friend	here	kind
feet	from	herself	king
fell	front	high	kitchen
felt	full	hill	kitten
fence	fun	him	kite
few	game	himself	knee
field	garden	his	knew
fighter	gave	hold	knife
figure	girl	hole	knock
fill	glad	home	know
finally	glass	hope	
find	glide	horse	
fine	goes	house	
finger	gold	how	
finish	gone	hundred	
fire	good	hungry	
first	got	hunt	
fish	grandfather	hurry	
fit	grandmother	hurt	
five	grass	ice	
flake	great	idea	
flash	grew	important	
flat	ground	indeed	
float	group	insect	
flood	grow	instead	
floor	guess	instrument	

SBA
Incentive Contract
calendar
for the month of:
_____

Child's Signature
_____
Parent's Signature

My Incentive Is:

When you have completed a daily activity, colour a

Day 1
Day 2
Day 3
Day 4
Day 5
Day 6
Day 7
Day 8
Day 9
Day 10

Day 11
Day 12
Day 13
Day 14
Day 15
Day 16
Day 17
Day 18
Day 19
Day 20

When you have completed ☐ minutes of reading, colour a

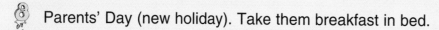

Fun Activity Ideas to Go Along with the Second Section!

1. Have a contest to name the provincial capital cities.

2. Play a game involving math like Racko, Uno®, or Monopoly®.

3. Go on a penny walk. On each corner, flip a penny to decide which way to go.

4. Paint a picture with lemon juice on white paper—hang it in a sunny window. In a few days, see what happens.

5. Plan a hike at a nearby wood lot.

6. Weed your garden.

7. Make a list of environmental problems. Decide how to help by changing things in your home (collect aluminum cans, etc.).

8. Parents' Day (new holiday). Take them breakfast in bed.

9. Hide an "I love you" note under your parents' pillows.

10. Make a date with your parents to attend something musical.

11. Find out what causes hiccups.

12. Cover a table in the yard with paper and paint a picture using pudding.

13. Visit a historical site.

14. Do chalk art on the front sidewalk.

15. Do a pioneer activity—brainstorm and be creative.

16. Have each family member write another family member a thank-you note.

17. Watch a science program on TV.

18. Take a counting walk: how many steps to the mailbox, how many to a friend's house, etc.

19. Make dessert tonight.

20. Give your pet a party. Invite its friends.

Mathematics—Addition and Subtraction

Follow the path. Write the answer.

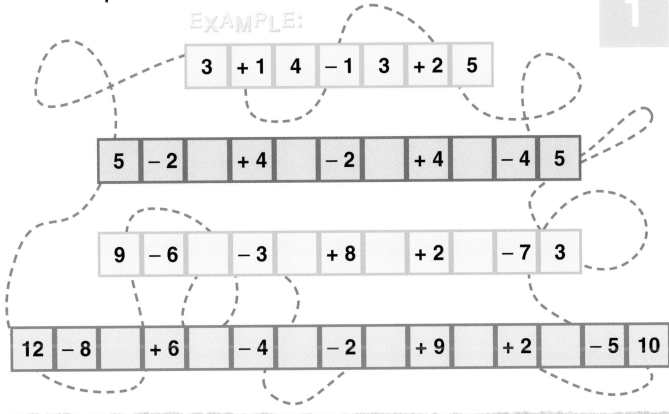

EXAMPLE:

3 + 1 | 4 | − 1 | 3 | + 2 | 5

5 | − 2 | | + 4 | | − 2 | | + 4 | | − 4 | 5

9 | − 6 | | − 3 | | + 8 | | + 2 | | − 7 | 3

12 | − 8 | | + 6 | | − 4 | | − 2 | | + 9 | | + 2 | | − 5 | 10

Phonics—Double Consonants

Some words end with two of the same consonant.

	off		fell		dress	stiff		shall	
class		stuff		glass		ball		mitt		hill

1. Write the word from the word box that rhymes with these words.

    _____   _____   _____

    - - - - - - - - - -   - - - - - - - - - -   - - - - - - - - - -

    bell _____   fill _____   puff _____

2. Write the missing word or words. Use words from the word box.

    Our _____ will put on a play for you.

    I _____ down and hurt my hand.

    Put some milk in my _____, please.

    Grab your _____ and let's play _____.

    The man is on top of the _____.

    Stand still and I will show you my new _____.

Day 1

Reading—Making Inferences

Read the sentences. Write *yes* if what the sentence says could really happen. Write *no* if what the sentence says could not really happen.

1. Jennifer wears a watch on her nose. _____

2. A robin flew to its nest in the tree. _____

3. Robert helped his father paint the fence. _____

4. Paul saw a striped cat swim across the river. _____

5. Mandy eats her lunch with a hammer and a saw. _____

6. We built a tunnel out of clay and rocks. _____

7. Birds use their beaks to fly. _____

8. Andy lost his tooth last night. _____

9. That cow is driving a bus! _____

10. My father works at school. _____

11. Bill flew in a spaceship to the sun. _____

12. The moose gave the frog a cookie. _____

Geography—Reading a Map to Locate Answers

Use the map to complete the sentences.

MAP

1. _____ Road runs north and south.

2. _____ Lake is between Trail Road and Jay Road.

3. _____ Mountains are the mountains in the south.

4. _____ Mountains are the mountains to the north.

5. _____ Road has the most cities on it.

6. _____ Town sounds spooky, _____ City sounds friendly, and _____ City sounds like you need to watch where you are going.

7. I would like to live on _____ Road!

Mathematics—Two-Digit Addition or Subtraction

84 − 42	37 − 13	69 + 20	18 − 4	57 + 21	70 + 30	87 − 36	146 + 13

22 − 16	24 − 11	10 − 10	23 + 12	19 − 10	26 + 22	35 + 33	99 − 34

43 + 43	91 + 6	15 − 9	12 + 2	88 + 10	49 − 38	16 + 3	287 − 12

Reading—Sequencing Parts of a Sentence in Order

Read the words in each group, and put them in the correct order. Place a period or a question mark at the end of each sentence. Read your sentence.

EXAMPLE:

__1__ It is fun

__3__ new friends.

__2__ to make

_____ Allie went

_____ know where

_____ Do you

_____ bones

_____ My dog

_____ can eat

_____ Ms. Hansen gave

_____ their papers

_____ the children

_____ car passed

_____ A green

_____ us

_____ Tanner are

_____ Grayson and

_____ brothers

_____ Matt has

_____ of cars

_____ four kinds

_____ kinds of cookies

_____ Denise ate

_____ four different

_____ love me

_____ and mom

_____ My dad

Reading—Following Directions
Read the paragraph, and then, follow the directions.

Denise likes to do many different things in the summer. Denise likes to sleep until eight o'clock. After she gets up, she likes to help her mother work in the garden for a while. Every day Denise likes to read and play with her friends. She likes to go swimming and hiking with her brothers. And most of all, she likes to ride her horse.

1. Underline the topic sentence.
2. Who does Denise go swimming with? Circle your answer.
3. Put an **X** on the time Denise gets up.
4. What do you think would be a good name for Denise's horse?

   _____

5. Name two things that might be growing in Denise's garden.

   _____

Word Study—Matching Word to Meaning

Read the sentences. Choose a word from the box below to complete the puzzle.

supper	camera
rake	cheese	agree
meat	microphone	

1. You talk into this to make your voice loud.
2. something you can eat
3. You take pictures with this.
4. You eat this at night.
5. People and mice like this.
6. My friend and I _____ on most things.
7. You do this to the leaves on your lawn.

Mathematics—Sequencing Numerals in Order

Connect the dots. Start with 597.

```
                                    .597
                                    .598
                           614.
                    613.              .599
             612.        615.            .600
          611.          616.               .601
        610.            617.                 .602
                        618.
609.        .608    .607       .606  .605  .604   .603
622.      .621    .620    619. _____ .631  .630   .629
     . 623
        .624        .625        .626     .627    .628
```

Word Study—Using Verbs Correctly

Choose the correct word from the box to complete the sentences.

1. The train will _____ .
   The train is _____ .
   The train has _____ .

   | **1.** stopped |
   | stopping |
   | stop |

2. The baby can _____ .
   See, the baby is _____ .
   The baby _____ .

   | **2.** clap |
   | clapped |
   | clapping |

3. The rabbit is _____ .
   The rabbit _____ .
   The rabbit can _____ .

   | **3.** hop |
   | hopped |
   | hopping |

4. Let's play _____ .
   I am _____ you.
   I _____ John.

   | **4.** tagged |
   | tagging |
   | tag |

Language—Writing Sentences with Given Words

Read the words in the box. Choose five words and write your own sentences. Use capital letters, periods, question marks, and exclamation points.

career	adult	complete	prepare
stranger	interested	college	during

1. _____
2. _____
3. _____
4. _____
5. _____

Reading—Sequencing Parts of Sentences in the Correct Order

Read the words in each group and put them in the correct order. Place a period at the end of each sentence. Read your sentence.

EXAMPLE:

__1__ My name	____ went to	____ blueberries
__3__ Jane Brown.	____ Today I	____ Rob's dog
__2__ is Mary	____ Grandma's	____ ate

____ a yellow bird	____ Grandpa's	____ likes to play
____ I saw three	____ puppies barked	____ Grayson
____ bugs and	____ at five fat cats	____ with his trains

Mathematics—Addition and Subtraction

Write the number fact families.

EXAMPLE:

1.

11

6   5

2.

4

5   9

3.

7

5   12

6 + 5 = 11	___ + ___ = ___	___ + ___ = ___
5 + 6 = 11	___ + ___ = ___	___ + ___ = ___
11 – 5 = 6	___ – ___ = ___	___ – ___ = ___
11 – 6 = 5	___ – ___ = ___	___ – ___ = ___

Phonics—Classifying Hard and Soft "C" Words

Read the words. Print the soft "c" words in the celery. Print the hard "c" words in the carrot.

cat	~~celery~~	once	rascal	excited	scene
cider	come	century	factor	dance	~~carrot~~
city	candy	actor	racoon	magic	sentence

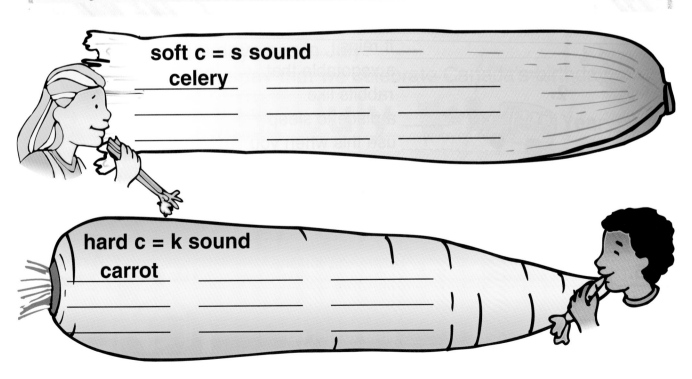

soft c = s sound
celery

hard c = k sound
carrot

Reading—Making Inferences

Read the stories. Decide what will happen next. Underline your answer.

1. Lori was about to take a big bite out of her ice cream. Denise bumped her arm.
   What will happen next?
   Lori will drink some milk.
   Lori will yell at Denise.
   Lori will get ice cream on her shorts.

2. Matt was playing tennis with Grayson. The sun was very hot. The boys' faces were getting too much sun.
   What will happen next?
   Grayson's and Matt's faces will get red.
   Matt will go home.
   Matt and Grayson will get cold.

Reading—Identifying and Matching Descriptions to Pictures

Look at the pictures. Read the sentences below. Write the sentence number in the box of the matching picture.

1. We are very rocky and high. Sheep and goats like to climb us.
2. People can go anywhere if they come to me first.
3. Here you can see many animals and people doing fun things.
4. You come to me on some days and learn.
5. This is something that every living thing needs.
6. I am a very special day in July.

Mathematics—Subtraction Facts
Subtract.

14	11	15	16	14	12	13	18
− 5	− 4	− 6	− 8	− 7	− 7	− 5	− 8

17	15	18	14	12	16	11	13
− 9	− 8	− 9	− 6	− 4	− 5	− 6	− 7

Reading—Context Clues
Write the words *who*, *what*, *when*, *why*, and *where* on the blanks to complete the sentences.

1. _____ will it be time to leave?

2. _____ wants to come with me?

3. _____ didn't you do your work?

4. _____ shall we go after the movie?

5. _____ time did you say it was?

6. _____ did you put my shoes and socks?

7. _____ must you leave so soon?

8. _____ are you doing now?

Reading—Word Usage

Use the words *went* or *gone* to finish these sentences. Remember, the word *gone* needs another word to help it, such as *has* or *have*.

EXAMPLE:

1. Tanner _____**went**_____ home after school.
2. Grayson has _____ shopping for a new coat.
3. Matt _____ with Denise to play.
4. We have _____ with Matt's mother all week.
5. Mother _____ to work this morning.
6. Allie has _____ around the corner.
7. Who has _____ on a trip before?
8. My aunt _____ skating on the ice.
9. I have _____ to bed.
10. He _____ around the world in an airplane.

Reading—Classifying Words under Headings

Write words or draw pictures for each category. Use words or pictures that begin or end with the letters on the left.

	Animals	Toys	Food	People
r	rat			
s		skate		
t			tomato	
l				little

Mathematics—Recognizing Time on a Clock

Circle the time that matches each clock.

8:30   12:45   1:45

10:15   8:10   9:15

6:00   12:00   12:30

8:25   6:25   5:08

5:30   6:40   5:40

1:05   12:00   12:05

Mathematics—Money: Making Change

Make one dollar's change in six different combinations.

EXAMPLE:

quarters	2
dimes	4
nickels	2
pennies	0
Total	$ 1.00

quarters	___
dimes	___
nickels	___
pennies	___
Total	$ ___

quarters	___
dimes	___
nickels	___
pennies	___
Total	$ ___

quarters	___
dimes	___
nickels	___
pennies	___
Total	$ ___

quarters	___
dimes	___
nickels	___
pennies	___
Total	$ ___

quarters	___
dimes	___
nickels	___
pennies	___
Total	$ ___

Reading—Identifying Words

Ask someone to say one of the words in each box. Circle the word that they say. When you finish, read all of the words on the page out loud.

course	floor
corner	fix
cost	fire
cook	five

instead	east
inside	else
into	easy
income	engine

begin	point
behind	plane
began	pickle
before	push

until	throw
unusually	through
unlace	those
unit	that

alarm	weather
adjust	wagon
alone	weave
afraid	weep

shape	year
snake	young
stone	yeast
stopped	yell

Word Study—Unscrambling Letters to Spell Words Correctly

Unscramble and write the missing words on the blank.

1. My mom always _____ me when I go to _____.
   ghus   **dbe**

2. Rob says that he _____ go home _____.
   sutm   **won**

3. The _____ swam in the _____ water.
   shif   **eedp**

4. My dad has to _____ our grass; it is too _____.
   tcu   **glno**

5. The cat chased _____ the mouse in his _____.
   frate   **ouhse**

6. Lori walks home from _____ and Matt _____.
   schloo   **diers**

7. A nickel is five _____, and a _____ is ten.
   tecsn   **iedm**

Mathematics—Addition with Regrouping

Add the ones first, and then, add the tens.

[1]	[ ]	[ ]	[ ]	[ ]	[ ]
63	47	19	55	24	88
+ 8	+ 8	+ 8	+ 9	+ 7	+ 6
71					

[ ]	[ ]	[ ]	[ ]	[ ]	[ ]
63	72	48	37	27	16
+ 9	+ 8	+ 4	+ 5	+ 6	+ 6

[ ]	[ ]	[ ]	[ ]	[ ]	[ ]
4	33	47	19	28	8
+ 16	+ 8	+ 7	+ 9	+ 7	+ 42

Phonics—Identifying the Long "oo" Sound and the Short "oo" Sound

Circle in green the words that have the (o͞o) sound like *tooth*. Circle in blue the words that have the (o͝o) sound like *hook*.

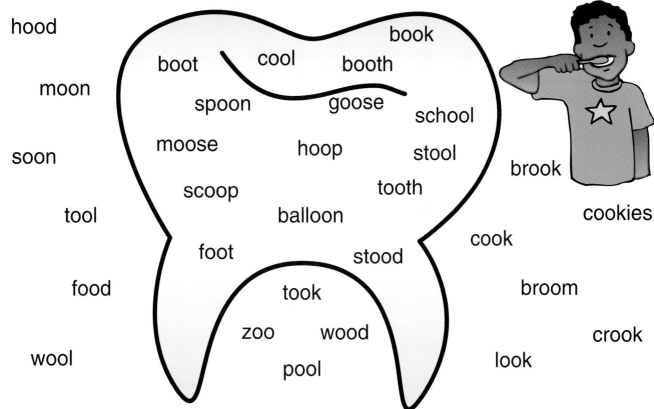

hood

moon

soon

tool

food

wool

boot   cool   booth   book

spoon   goose   school

moose   hoop   stool   brook

scoop   tooth   cookies

balloon   cook

foot   stood

took   broom

zoo   wood   crook

pool   look

Reading—Noting Details

Read the story about Max and Joy. Write an *M* by the things that describe Max and a *J* by the things that describe Joy. Write a *B* if it describes both of them.

Max and Joy are twins. They have brown eyes and black hair. They are seven years old and go to school. Max likes math, and Joy likes to read. They both like to go outside to play. Joy likes to play ball. Max likes to run and play tag. Joy likes to ride her bike, while Max feeds his pet dog.

_____ 1. has brown eyes   ___ 7. are seven

_____ 2. likes to read   ___ 8. likes to run

_____ 3. likes to ride bikes   ___ 9. likes math

_____ 4. likes to play ball   ___ 10. has black hair

_____ 5. has a pet   ___ 11. likes to go outside

_____ 6. are twins   ___ 12. go to school

Science—Spelling Things Correctly That Are Solids, Liquids, and Gases

Matter is all around us. It can be *solid* like wood, *liquid* like milk, or a *gas* like steam. **Unscramble the words, and fill in the blanks.**

1. Ice is a _____. When it melts, it is a _____.
   dliso   **ildqui**

2. I have no shape. You can feel me when the wind blows. _____.
   asg

3. Matter is what things are made of. It has three forms: _____, _____, and _____.
   sga
   dqiiul   **osdil**

4. _____ can be big or little, soft or hard.
   tertaM

5. _____ takes the shape of what you put it in.
   qidiLu

6. Rocks are _____.
   odlsi

7. You can take a bath in this matter: _____.
   ilqidu

8. Air is a _____.
   sag

Mathematics—Money: Counting Coins

Count the money. Write the total on the line. Colour the item that costs more.

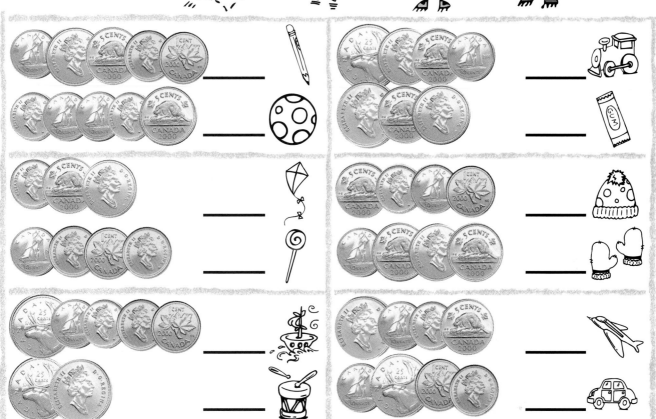

Phonics—Identifying Long and Short Vowel Sounds

Listen to the vowel sounds. If the word has a short vowel sound, put an *S* on the line. If the vowel sound is long, put an *L* on the line.

EXAMPLE:

just	**S**	clock	____	name	____
cute	**L**	slow	____	truck	____
nice	____	cape	____	help	____
road	____	clue	____	chip	____
ship	____	apple	____	trike	____
shot	____	seed	____	shame	____
left	____	gum	____	goat	____
slam	____	sweet	____	read	____
take	____	lime	____	lamp	____
leaf	____	light	____	mule	____

Reading—Main Idea

Choose a word from the box below to answer the riddles.

| dew | giraffe | crib | skunk | mouse | rope | glue | moose | broom |

1. Cleo is black and white. He can make a terrible smell.
Cleo is a _____.

2. Sweep the floor with me.
I am a _____.

3. Rick is small and grey. He has a long tail. He likes cheese.
Rick is a _____.

4. Tiny has a long neck and brown spots on her body. She eats leaves off the trees.
Tiny is a _____.

5. You can stick things together with me.
I am _____.

6. You can tie things up with me. I can be thick or thin.
I am a _____.

7. Harry lives in the forest by a pond. He eats grass on the bottom of the pond and has big antlers.
Harry is a _____.

8. You can find me on the grass on cool mornings.
I am _____.

9. Babies sleep in me. I have four legs, but I cannot walk.
I am a _____.

Reading—Sequencing Sentences

Read the sentences and put an X next to what happened first.

_____ I planted seeds.
_____ The flowers grew.

_____ I did my work.
_____ I must do my work.

_____ Katie spent all of her money.
_____ Katie has a lot of money.

_____ Kirt starts his car.
_____ Kirt stops his car.

_____ I brushed my teeth.
_____ I put toothpaste on my brush.

_____ Our snowman is tall.
_____ Our snowman melted.

_____ I put my shoes on.
_____ I put on my socks.

_____ Mom baked a cake.
_____ I ate a piece of cake.

Mathematics—Two-Column Addition

[1]	☐	☐	☐	☐	☐
32	28	70	44	57	26
11	14	99	2	32	33
+ 19	+ 4	+ 12	+ 38	+ 89	+ 44
62					

☐	☐	☐	☐	☐	☐
81	22	67	81	74	6
38	9	45	8	33	24
+ 64	+ 19	+ 15	+ 8	+ 17	+ 36

Word Study—Alphabetical Order

Put these words in alphabetical order. They are r-controlled vowel words.

her	card	jerk	turn	march
word	are	burn	more	store
bird	third	dark	part	first

1. _____
2. _____
3. _____
4. _____
5. _____

6. _____
7. _____
8. _____
9. _____
10. _____

11. _____
12. _____
13. _____
14. _____
15. _____

Word Study—Recognizing Syllables

Syllables *be*, *a*, *re*, *ex*, and *de* are common beginning syllables. Read the words in each box. Circle the syllable common to each word. Then, choose the correct word to write in the blank.

ⓐfraid	ⓐlive	ⓐhead
remove	repair	renew
exchange	exhibit	exit
before	because	became
about	around	alarming
decoy	decline	decree
receive	recall	recess
behind	belief	belong
depend	deposit	describe
explore	expert	export

1. I will walk __**ahead**__ of you.

2. Will you please _____ my shoes?

3. Mom will _____ this dress for a skirt.

4. After ten years of school, my sister _____ a doctor.

5. This story was _____ some strange animals.

6. The king sent a _____ from the palace.

7. The children like _____ time.

8. I _____ to the school chorus.

9. We will _____ our money in the bank.

10. Let's _____ this cave.

Language—Creative Writing

Write a story called "My Favourite Month of the Year."

_____

_____

_____

_____

_____

_____

_____

Mathematics—Problem Solving

Solve the problems below.

1. Lori has 13 roses. She sold 9 of them. How many roses does she have left to sell?
_____ roses

2. Grayson can walk 2 kilometres in 1 hour. How many kilometres can he walk in 2 hours?
_____ kilometres

3. Matt has 14 toy cars, and Tanner has 10 toy cars. How many more cars does Matt have than Tanner?
_____ cars

4. Twenty-eight tigers were in a tent. Twenty-one went outside. How many stayed in the tent?
_____ tigers

5. Denise has 9 teddy bears. Allie has 6 dolls, and Lori has 3 balls. How many toys do the girls have in all?
_____ toys

Phonics—Using "ph" Words Correctly in Sentences

The letters *ph* make the sound of (f). Read the sentences, and choose the correct word from the word box to write on the blanks.

1. What is your _____ number?
2. We saw _____ at the zoo.
3. Allie wrote the letters of the _____.
4. Our team will get a _____.
5. Andy is my neat _____.
6. Lori likes to sing into the _____.
7. Matt is a great _____.

Word Box

trophy
phone
nephew
alphabet
elephants
microphone
photographer

Word Study—Using Compound Words

Choose the right word for each sentence.

1. Denise is one of my favourite _____.

   classmates   rainbows   buttermilk

2. Allie likes to go _____ in the sand.

   footstool   barefoot   football

3. It rains a lot during _____.

   playtime   springtime   lunchtime

4. Put the _____ on to set the table.

   tablecloth   washcloth   pitchfork

5. Our family ate crab at _____.

   dinnertime   snowflake   shoelace

6. I like to collect _____ at the beach.

   storybooks   seashells   butterflies

Word Study—Matching Words to Meanings

Draw a line from the word in the first column to the words that best describe it.

1. milk   a farm animal
2. penny   something to drink
3. sandwich   a planet
4. ice cream   money
5. cow   usually very cold
6. yellow   a type of tent
7. hammer   a pet
8. Earth   a colour
9. teepee   a tool
10. dog   something to eat

Mathematics—Place Value

Read the words, and then, write the correct numeral in the blank.

EXAMPLE:

1. 2 hundreds, 8 tens, 3 ones = **283**

   427 = **4** hundreds, **2** tens, **7** ones.

   193 = _____ hundreds, _____ tens, _____ ones.

   7 hundreds, 2 tens, 0 ones = _____

2. 24 = _____ tens, _____ ones

   93 = _____ ones, _____ tens

   30 = _____ tens, _____ ones

3. 98 = _____ ones, _____ tens

   34 = _____ tens, _____ ones

   6 = _____ tens, _____ ones

4. 6 tens, 4 ones = _____

   2 ones, 8 tens = _____

5. 9 ones, 7 tens = _____

   3 tens, 9 ones = _____

Reading—Classifying Words into Categories

Write the words from the word box in the correct category.

Animals

Toys

Food

Animals	Toys	Food
1. _____	1. _____	1. _____
2. _____	2. _____	2. _____
3. _____	3. _____	3. _____
4. _____	4. _____	4. _____
5. _____	5. _____	5. _____
6. _____	6. _____	6. _____

cow	blocks	rabbit	beans	bread	monkey
ball	sled	kite	horse	meat	donkey
corn	cherry	lion	potatoes	train	doll

Language—Word Referents

Read the sentences. Draw a circle around the word or words that the underlined word stands for.

EXAMPLE:

1. If you will be home (Friday), I will see you <u>then</u>.
2. The fruit is really good; <u>it</u> tastes sweet.
3. Joe and Henry run fast; <u>they</u> won the race.
4. When we found the park, Dad said, "Let's eat <u>here</u>."
5. Mary plays the piano; <u>she</u> plays very well.
6. I watered the flowers and put <u>them</u> on the bench.
7. Danny took the dog outside; he left the cat <u>there</u>, too.
8. The fish swam in the pond; <u>it</u> ate a bug.
9. "Hi there," said my friend when <u>he</u> came to my house.
10. I know some lizards change <u>their</u> colour.

Language—Descriptive Vocabulary

Colour your favourite drink in one glass and your least favourite drink in the other. Write at least three words that describe each.

Mathematics—Subtraction with Regrouping

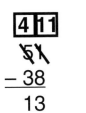

EXAMPLE:

```
 4 11
 5 1
-38
 13
```

```
[  ]
 75
-26
```

```
[  ]
 82
-37
```

```
[  ]
 27
-19
```

```
[  ]
 70
-24
```

```
[  ]
 41
-16
```

```
[  ]
 65
- 9
```

```
[  ]
 83
-24
```

```
[  ]
 95
-78
```

```
[  ]
 56
-17
```

```
[  ]
 22
- 8
```

```
[  ]
 38
-19
```

```
[  ]
 81
- 6
```

```
[  ]
 54
-39
```

```
[  ]
 64
-18
```

```
[  ]
 35
-16
```

```
[  ]
 87
-48
```

```
[  ]
 60
-36
```

Word Study—Recognizing Words Found in Other Words

Circle all of the small words that you can find in these words.

EXAMPLE: toward   forest

1. statement
2. spend
3. bonnet
4. penmanship
5. friend
6. spring
7. kingdom
8. visitor
9. coldness

10. infant
11. behind
12. kittens
13. twinkled
14. carpet
15. pinch
16. canyon
17. fellow
18. strawberry

19. storage
20. million
21. identify
22. balloon
23. rabbit
24. chocolate
25. sentence
26. another
27. microphone

Reading—Noting Detail

Read each sentence and mark the correct one. Pay close attention to the commas.

1. Denise wanted <u>five</u> things in her lunch.
   _____ Denise got an apple, cake, an orange, carrots, and candy for her lunch.
   _____ Denise got an applecake, an orange, carrots, and candy for her lunch.

2. Grayson saw <u>three</u> children at the park.
   _____ Alex Lee, Henry, and John were playing at the park.
   _____ Alex, Lee, Henry, and John were playing at the park.

3. Lori has <u>four</u> things in her room.
   _____ She has a basketball, a teddy bear, and a book.
   _____ She has a basket, a ball, a teddy bear, and a book.

Word Study—Identifying Puzzle Words

Write these summer words in the boxes. Make sure they fit.

swimming

fishing

baseball

football

camping

vacation

f
u
n

biking

fun

play

(water) skiing

Mathematics—Money: Counting Money

Count the money. Write the amount on the line.

1.  _____ ¢

2.  _____ ¢

3.  _____ ¢

4.  _____ ¢

5. _____ ¢

Language—Forming Questions from Sentences

Change the order of each telling sentence to form a question. Remember the question mark.

EXAMPLE: **The busy mailman is leaving. → Is the busy mailman leaving?**

1. The old man is Gary's grandfather.

_____

2. Apples are red, round, and juicy.

_____

3. She can ride her shiny, new bike.

_____

4. I am going to ride a black horse.

_____

Reading—Context Clues

Fill in the blank with the correct word to complete the sentence.

1. Trains travel on railroad _____.
   tracks   trucks   turtles
2. My grandpa reached the _____ of 100 years.
   ant   age   ape
3. Denise likes to _____ beauty salon.
   peel   plate   play
4. My mom put on a _____ dress for the day.
   biggest   lovely   lately
5. The grass turns green in the _____.
   sprang   spring   sprung
6. This _____ of the house is not warm.
   section   station   nation
7. The _____ was shining in my eyes.
   bright   flight   light
8. A horse kicks with its _____ legs.
   blind   hind   mind
9. The fence was made of _____.
   wire   tire   fire
10. I will pay the _____ so I can ride the bus.
    rare   square   fare

Reading—Following Written Directions

Follow the directions to make a picture.

3.   .C

R.
D.   5.   9.
Z.

1. Draw a line from 3 to 5.
2. Draw a line from 3 to C to 9.
3. Draw a line from 3 to D.
4. Draw a line from D to Z to 5.
5. Draw a line from Z to 9.
6. Draw a line from 3 to R to D.
7. Draw a line from 3 to Z.
8. Colour and draw the things that you would take camping.

Mathematics—Locating Facts of 11 and 12

Draw two straight lines to divide the square so each area totals . . .

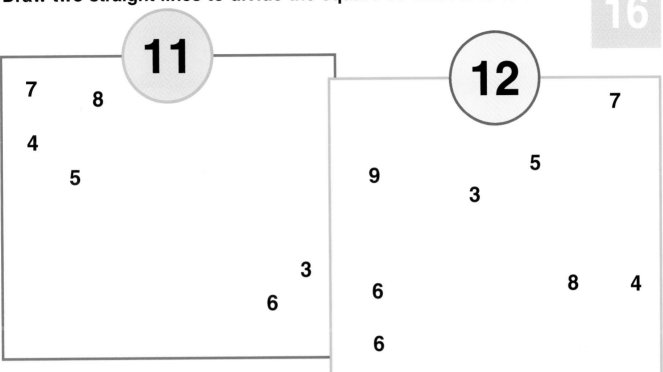

Language—Abbreviations

To abbreviate a word means to shorten it. Match the abbreviation to the word.

EXAMPLE:

December	Dr.	Mister	Canada
Doctor	g	October	km
Thursday	Dec.	kilometre	Mr.
gram	Jan.	Ave.	Avenue
January	Thurs.	Can.	Oct.
metre	Junior	Saturday	Sr.
March	Wed.	Senior	St.
Jr.	m	Monday	Mon.
centimetre	cm	Captain	Capt.
Wednesday	Mar.	street	Sat.

Language—Punctuation

Read the sentences. Put a (.), (?), or (!) at the end of the sentence.

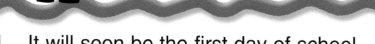

1. It will soon be the first day of school_____
2. Will Judy ride her bike to school this year_____
3. Have you had a fun summer vacation_____
4. My family went on a camping trip to the beach_____
5. Ann's sister will be starting school this year_____
6. What day will school start for you_____
7. Do you know the name of your new teacher_____
8. Amy's mother is going to go to school this fall_____
9. She will learn to be a teacher_____
10. Have you gone anywhere before_____
11. Where are you going, and how will you get there_____
12. Have fun_____

Word Study—Alphabetical Order

Look at the parts of the bird, and then, write the parts in alphabetical order.

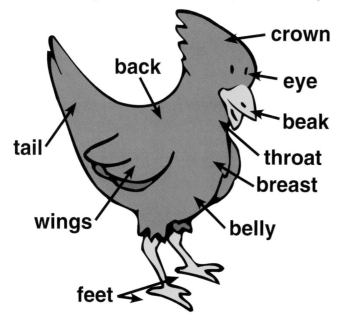

crown
back
eye
beak
tail
throat
breast
wings
belly
feet

1. _____
2. _____
3. _____
4. _____
5. _____
6. _____
7. _____
8. _____
9. _____
10. _____

Mathematics—Addition and Subtraction with Regrouping

Add or subtract. Be sure to start with the ones column.

33	62	19	53	67	58
+ 18	− 28	+ 20	− 5	− 38	+ 24

44	34	72	75	47	81
− 18	− 9	+ 9	− 47	− 14	+ 11

31	28	46	31	54	7
− 21	+ 14	− 6	− 16	+ 27	+ 33

Language—Using Verbs in Sentences

Use the correct word from the box in each sentence. Some words need the helper *has*, *have*, or *had*.

was	is	Did	saw	gave
were	are	done	seen	given

1. I _____ my cousin Jamie.
2. Where _____ you going?
3. I have _____ many bugs crawling.
4. _____ you find your green pencil?
5. The one I lost _____ green.
6. That _____ the one I want.
7. He _____ me his new bike.
8. We have _____ all the candy away.
9. You _____ great!
10. He has _____ it once again.

has

have

had

www.summerbridgeactivities.com   69   © Summer Bridge Activities™ ✹ 2–3

Reading—Context Clues

Write the correct word from the box to finish the sentences.

EXAMPLE:

Word Box

longest
greenest
nicest
wider
closing
driving
softest
wiser
talking
~~moved~~
taking
wanted
waved
waited
talking

1. We _____**moved**_____ close to my grandma's.

2. It took us the _____ time to get there.

3. I took my turn _____.

4. I said, "It is _____ us too long."

5. The streets are getting _____.

6. The _____ part of this whole thing will be _____ to Grandma.

7. Mom _____ a bigger house.

8. We saw my cousin. He _____ at us.

9. He _____ for us to come.

10. We were all _____ at once!

Language—Creative Writing

Pretend you live in a tree house. Write a story describing what it is like to live in your tree house.

_____

_____

_____

_____

_____

_____

_____

_____

_____

_____

Mathematics—Place Value

Circle the number if:

EXAMPLE:

7 is in the ones place
34 (177) (67) 76
84 (27) 42 (7) 16

6 is in the hundreds place			
629	426	601	47
926	682	62	26
636	426	600	660

5 is in the tens place			
126	54	151	555
38	185	250	58
859	50	725	255

9 is in the ones place			
79	429	924	609
191	509	313	94
889	69	74	209

4 is in the hundreds place			
1 423	484		124
2 642	1 600		432
3 046	4 422		144

3 is in the tens place			
231	722	38	29
1 639	63	530	3
333	32	23	16

0 is in the tens place		
50	101	609
1 406	10	804
36	420	99

7 is in the ones place		
27	147	607
38	78	447
99	997	1 007

1 is in the tens place			
1	211	184	1 121
71	17	130	6 191
140	100	501	122

Word Study—Recognizing Unusual Plurals

Change the spelling of the underlined words to make them plural.

mice
elves
leaves
knives
feet
teeth
geese
~~men~~

EXAMPLE:

1. one <u>man</u> or two _____**men**_____
2. one <u>tooth</u> or three _____
3. one <u>leaf</u> or four _____
4. one <u>goose</u> or five _____
5. one <u>knife</u> or two _____
6. one <u>mouse</u> or six _____
7. one <u>elf</u> or four _____
8. one <u>foot</u> or nine _____

Language—Writing Questions and Sentences Using Given Words

Read the words in the word box. Then, write three telling sentences and three question sentences. Use a word from the word box in each of your sentences.

Word Box

silence
attention
calmly
famous
honour
strange
moment
station
million
free
sniffed
shiver

1. _____

2. _____

3. _____

4. _____

5. _____

6. _____

Language—Adjectives

Words that *describe* tell something about other words in a sentence. Some words describe how things look. Some words describe how things sound. Some words describe how things feel or how things taste. Circle the describing words in the sentences.

1. Ella has on a pretty blue dress.
2. We left for our trip on a cloudy day.
3. The shrill whistle hurt my ears.
4. That sad child must be lost.
5. Joe likes a soft pillow.
6. The sour lemon made my mouth water.
7. Our class climbed a steep hill.
8. The door made a screechy noise.
9. The hot, wet sand felt good on our feet.
10. That fluffy yellow kitten is mine.

EXAMPLE:

The (big), (red) wagon rolled down the hill.

Big and *red* tell how the wagon looks.

Mathematics—Metric Measurement

Use a metric ruler to measure the lines between the dots. Write the measurements in the boxes and add them together.

☐ + ☐ + ☐ = _____ centimetres

☐ + ☐ + ☐ = _____ centimetres

☐ + ☐ + ☐ = _____ centimetres

Phonics—"Y" as a Vowel

Sometimes *Y* is a vowel. Circle the word that is spelled correctly in each row.

EXAMPLE:

(sunny)   suny   sunnie

1.	babi	babby	baby
2.	pretty	pritty	prety
3.	kary	cary	carry
4.	sily	silly	selly
5.	whi	why	whhy
6.	try	trie	trhi
7.	bodie	body	boddy
8.	funy	funnie	funny
9.	crie	cri	cry
10.	twenty	twenny	twienty

Reading—Recognizing the Speaker in Sentences

Who is talking in the following sentences? Write the name of the person talking on the line.

1. Grayson said, "Tanner, you need to go to bed." _____**Grayson**_____
2. "Is this your book, Allie?" asked Denise. _____
3. Allie replied, "No, Denise, it is not my book." _____
4. The dog barked, "This is my house, cat, go away!"
   _____
5. "Would you please go to the store for me?" Mother asked.
   _____
6. "Denise," said Father, "Mr. Fredrickson wants us to go to the zoo with him. Lori, would you like to go?" _____
7. "I want to eat now," I said. "I cannot wait." _____
8. "Is it hard to ride a bike, Grandpa?" asked Matt. _____
9. "No," said Grandpa. "Not if you practise a lot." _____
10. "Come over and play with me, Denise," yelled Allie.
    _____

Mathematics—Connecting Letters and Numerals to Make a Shape

Use a ruler to connect the dots between matching numerals and letters. See what design you make. Colour the design.

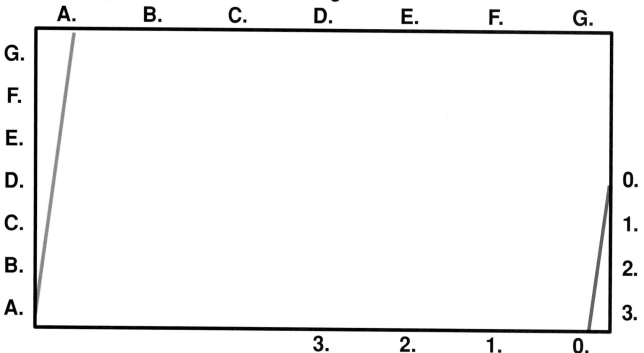

Write the time, or draw the hands.

9:25

_____ : _____

6:35

one hour
later

4:50

_____ : _____

one hour
later

11:10

_____ : _____

Word Study—Homonyms

Write the homonym of the underlined word.

EXAMPLE:

1. Did you <u>write</u> down the _____ **right** _____ answer?
2. My dad <u>ate</u> _____ pancakes for breakfast.
3. I can<u>not</u> tie a _____ with this rope.
4. Don only <u>won</u> _____ game.
5. <u>Would</u> you cut some _____ for the stove?
6. <u>Be</u> careful or that _____ will sting you!
7. I <u>knew</u> that I would get some _____ shoes.
8. Our <u>maid</u> has already _____ my bed.
9. At the circus, we saw a man fight a <u>bear</u> with his _____ hands.
10. Stay <u>here</u> and you will _____ the bell when it rings.

bee	**hear**	**bare**	**eight**	**knot**
~~**right**~~	**one**	**new**	**wood**	**made**

Word Study—Using Suffixes

Add *-less* or *-ness* to the base word in the sentence.

EXAMPLE:

1. I took the __home**less**__ kitten to my house.
2. The children were very __rest__ today.
3. He was very __care__ with matches.
4. Rob had lost so many teeth, he looked __tooth__.
5. The __friendli__ of the people made us feel at home.
6. Trying to train my dog to sit up is __hope__.
7. The baby loves the __soft__ of her blanket.
8. The __loud__ of the noise made me jump.
9. Her __happi__ showed on her face.
10. My __forgetful__ is going to get me in trouble.

Mathematics—Symmetry

Draw the other half of the picture to match.

Words to Sound, Read, and Spell

lace	many	must	pair
laid	mark	myself	paper
lake	mask	name	parent
land	match	near	park
large	material	need	part
last	may	neighbour	party
late	mean	nest	past
later	meant	never	path
laugh	meat	new	pay
laughter	medium	next	pencil
lay	meet	nice	people
lead	mention	night	perhaps
lean	mess	noise	person
learn	message	north	phone
leave	middle	nose	pick
left	might	note	picnic
leg	mile	nothing	picture
lesson	milk	notice	piece
letter	million	number	place
life	mind	off	plan
lift	mine	offer	plane
light	minute	often	plant
like	moment	old	plate
line	money	oldest	play
list	monkey	once	please
listen	monster	only	pocket
little	moon	open	point
live	more	order	police
long	morning	other	poor
look	most	our	porch
lost	mother	out	post
lot	mountain	over	power
loud	mouse	owl	present
love	mouth	own	pretend
low	move	pack	pretty
made	movie	page	princess
mail	much	paid	principal
main	mud	pail	probably
make	music	paint	problem

Words to Sound, Read, and Spell

proud	row	shine	snake
puddle	rub	shirt	snow
pull	rubber	shoe	soft
punch	rug	shook	sold
push	rule	shop	solve
queen	run	short	some
question	sad	should	song
quickly	safe	shoulder	soon
quiet	said	shout	sorry
quite	sail	show	sound
rabbit	same	shut	soup
race	sand	shy	south
rail	sank	sick	space
rain	save	side	speak
raise	saw	sigh	special
ran	say	sign	speed
reach	school	silly	spell
read	sea	since	spent
ready	seat	sing	spoon
really	second	sink	sport
reason	see	sister	spot
receive	seed	six	spread
record	seem	size	
remember	self	skate	
report	sell	skill	
rest	send	skin	
rich	sent	skip	
ride	sentence	sky	
right	seven	slap	
ring	several	sled	
river	sew	sleep	
road	shack	slid	
rock	shade	slip	
rocket	shake	slow	
roll	shall	slowly	
roller	shape	small	
room	sharp	smart	
rope	sheep	smell	
round	shelf	smile	

My Incentive Is:

SBA
Incentive Contract
calendar
for the month of:

Child's Signature

Parent's Signature

When you have completed a daily activity, colour a

Day 1
Day 2
Day 3
Day 4
Day 5
Day 6
Day 7

Day 8
Day 9
Day 10
Day 11
Day 12
Day 13
Day 14
Day 15

When you have completed ☐ minutes of reading, colour a

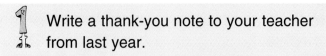
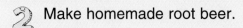

Discover Something New!

Fun Activity Ideas to Go Along with the Third Section!

1. Write a thank-you note to your teacher from last year.

2. Make homemade root beer.

3. Visit the library. Research an occupation.

4. Visit someone in your chosen occupation.

5. Have a neighbourhood barbecue.

6. Contact your city hall and do some volunteer work.

7. Try a midweek campout.

8. Go to a farm and feed the animals.

9. Plan a neighbourhood bicycle Olympics.

10. Share your garden produce with your neighbours.

11. Remember your times tables. Practise.

12. Have a marble tournament.

13. Make and fly a paper airplane.

14. Visit a fish hatchery.

15. Have a backyard breakfast.

Mathematics—Using Symbols to Compare Quantities

Write the signs for greater than (>), less than (<), or equal to (=) in the circles.

EXAMPLE:

7 + 7 $<$ 15   9 + 7 ◯ 16   8 + 9 ◯ 18

8 + 6 $=$ 14   13 – 4 ◯ 10   10 – 4 ◯ 6

15 $>$ 1 + 9   16 + 4 ◯ 17   17 – 9 ◯ 8

3 + 3 $=$ 2 + 4   11 ◯ 3 + 9   4 ◯ 12 – 8

8 + 9 ◯ 9 + 8   5 + 8 ◯ 6 + 7   15 – 5 ◯ 13 – 4

11 – 4 ◯ 6 + 2   12 – 6 ◯ 6 + 6   18 – 8 ◯ 8 + 8

12 – 1 ◯ 12 – 6   10 + 1 ◯ 4 + 7   9 + 3 ◯ 14 – 7

9 ◯ 13 – 5   5 + 9 ◯ 16   14 – 8 ◯ 5 + 1

Reading—Noting Detail

Read the story. Complete the picture to go with the story.

Mary planted flowers in each pot. They grew fast. She put the flowers all in a row. The white flower was in the middle. The purple flower was second. The orange flower was not first. The yellow flower was last. Where was the pink flower? Where does the orange flower go?

Science—The Weather

Weather is all around us. Sun, air, and water all work together to make different kinds of weather. Use the words in the box to write three different weather sentences.

1. _____
   _____

2. _____
   _____

3. _____
   _____

clouds
rain
fog
flood
snowstorms
lightning
thunder
tornado
wind
sleet
hail
ice
sun

Word Study—Adding Suffixes to Base Words

Add -ed, -ing, or -er to the following base words. Words that end in -n, -g, and -p may need an additional letter. Those ending in -e may change, also.

EXAMPLE:

rake	jump	hug	cook	skate
raked	_____	_____	_____	_____
raking	_____	_____	_____	_____

wrap	sneeze	pop	walk	smile
_____	_____	_____	_____	_____
_____	_____	_____	_____	_____

Mathematics—Metric Measurement

Use a metric ruler to find the length of each object.

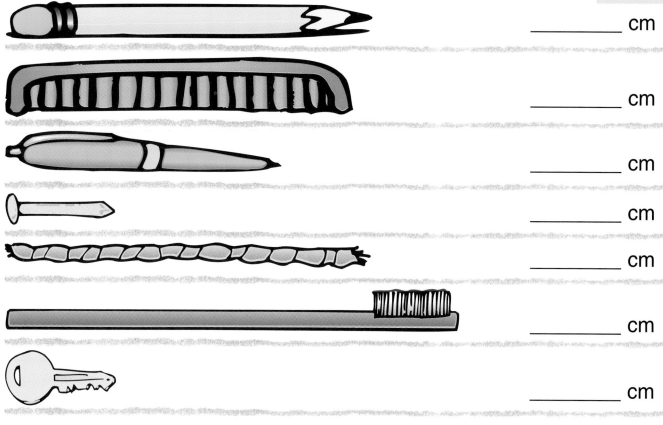

_____ cm

_____ cm

_____ cm

_____ cm

_____ cm

_____ cm

_____ cm

Language—Verbs

"Doing" words are called *verbs*. Some doing words mean *to do it now or later*; others mean *we already did it*. Put the doing words on the correct ladder. EXAMPLE:

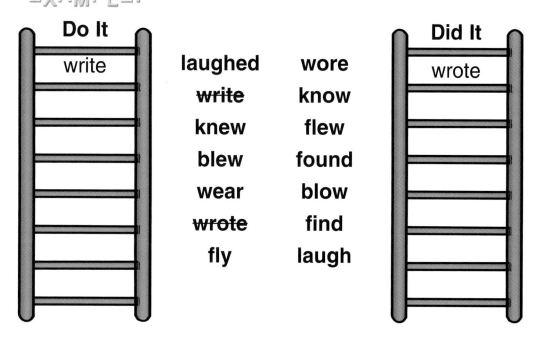

Do It

write

laughed   wore

~~write~~   know

knew   flew

blew   found

wear   blow

~~wrote~~   find

fly   laugh

Did It

wrote

Language—Capitalization and Punctuation

Write these sentences correctly. Do not forget the capital letters, periods, question marks, commas, and quotation marks.

1. randy has five pets: a dog cat rabbit and two mice

   -

2. do bluebirds eat seeds insects and plants

   -

3. would you please go to the store for me asked grayson

   -

4. my name is allie and I like candy

   -

Word Study—Classifying Antonyms, Homonyms, and Synonyms

Write the words under the correct heading.	(opposite) **Antonyms**	(sound alike) **Homonyms**	(mean the same) **Synonyms**
EXAMPLE: would wood		would wood	
1. high low			
2. pile heap			
3. weight wait			
4. blend mix			
5. empty full			
6. difficult hard			
7. rain reign			
8. cool warm			
9. crawl creep			
10. groan grown			

Mathematics—Fractions

Colour the correct fraction for each picture.

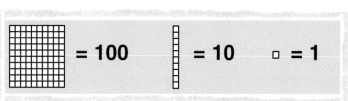

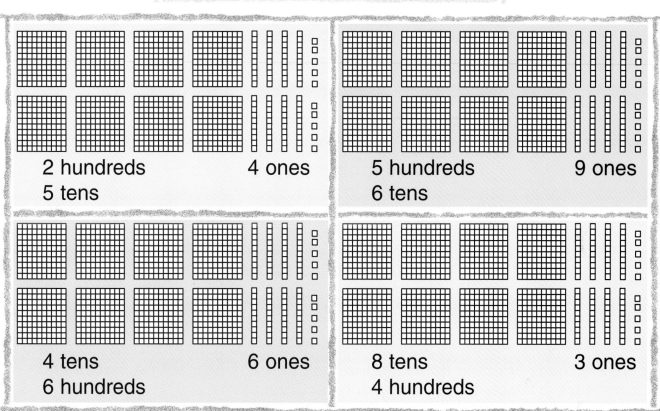

2 hundreds   4 ones
5 tens

5 hundreds   9 ones
6 tens

4 tens   6 ones
6 hundreds

8 tens   3 ones
4 hundreds

Phonics—Initial Consonant Substitution

Read each word. Look at the underlined letter or letters. Change the letter or letters in each word to make a new word. Read them to your parents.

EXAMPLE:

<u>t</u>ake   **bake**   <u>p</u>ress _____   <u>w</u>ell _____

<u>pr</u>ize _____   <u>d</u>ove _____   <u>q</u>uick _____

<u>r</u>ise _____   <u>c</u>ost _____   w<u>i</u>sh _____

th<u>o</u>se _____   sh<u>e</u>ll _____   <u>s</u>hip _____

<u>t</u>rue _____   b<u>u</u>d _____   <u>tr</u>uck _____

Reading—Sequence

Read the story. Then, number the events in the order that they happened.

It had snowed for three days. When it stopped, the snow was so deep Tom and Don could not get out through the door of the cabin. The men had to climb out of the upstairs window in order to get outside. They spent hours shovelling the snow away from the cabin door. At last, they were able to get the door open.

(   ) The men climbed out of the window.

(   ) It snowed for three days.

(   ) Don and Tom got the door open.

(   ) The men shovelled snow for hours.

Language—Creativity

There are many kinds of doors that belong to many interesting places and things: cars, houses, barns, bedrooms, and basements.

Think of a door that could lead you to an interesting place or a strange thing. Draw a picture of your door and what is behind it.

Mathematics—Three-Digit Subtraction

758	410	894	978	879	646
− 126	− 310	− 251	− 165	− 704	− 16

785	583	957	683	896	923
− 223	− 161	− 140	− 611	− 840	− 111

686	349	867	539	767	297
− 255	− 104	− 36	− 39	− 10	− 177

Language—Completing Analogies

Write the correct word from the Word Bank.

EXAMPLE:

1. Car is to road as boat is to _____ **lake** _____.

2. Cloud is to sky as worm is to _____.

3. City is to buildings as forest is to _____.

4. Knob is to door as pane is to _____.

5. Cub is to bear as calf is to _____.

6. Bus is to car as airplane is to _____.

7. Quack is to duck as meow is to _____.

8. Begin is to start as end is to _____.

9. Uncle is to aunt as father is to _____.

10. Squirrel is to nut as cow is to _____.

Word Bank

cat

ground

hay

window

mother

~~lake~~

trees

cow

jet

stop

Day 4

Word Study—Spelling Words Correctly

Finish writing the correct word in each sentence by changing the last letter and adding the correct ending.

EXAMPLE:

Word List

- drier
- happiest
- easier
- tried
- carried
- flies
- worries
- ~~funniest~~

1. Wanda showed me the __funn~~y~~iest__ picture.

2. My clothes are _____dry_____ than yours.

3. That bird _____fly_____ south for the winter.

4. Joe _____worry_____ about his sick friend.

5. My book is _____easy_____ to read than yours.

6. This was my _____happy_____ birthday ever!

7. Pete _____carry_____ his books to school.

8. I _____try_____ to get the door unstuck.

Phonics—Word Families

Find these *-ack*, *-ick*, *-ock*, *-uck*, and *-eck* words in the word search puzzle. Circle them. Then, fill in the blanks with words from the word box.

w	b	a	c	k	z	y	r
r	s	t	u	c	k	w	o
e	k	o	k	o	m	i	c
c	c	r	b	s	q	c	k
k	i	s	p	e	c	k	d
l	l	u	c	k	c	c	u
p	e	c	k	a	x	w	c
y	l	u	p	c	h	d	k

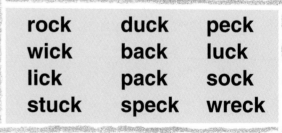

rock	duck	peck
wick	back	luck
lick	pack	sock
stuck	speck	wreck

The _____
put her _____
on the _____.

Mathematics—Three-Digit Addition

324	973	777	206	88	548
+ 125	+ 24	+ 112	+ 132	+ 171	+ 241

420	623	621	230	175	422
+ 337	+ 125	+ 126	+ 362	+ 113	+ 561

803	603	9	300	540	921
+ 104	+ 292	+ 600	+ 500	+ 7	+ 157

Word Study—Spelling

Is the underlined word spelled right or wrong? Mark your answer. Correctly write the words that are spelled wrong.

EXAMPLE:

		right	wrong
1.	Marcus has a new <u>electrik</u> car.	electric	○ ●
2.	Sara takes the fast <u>trane</u> to work.	_____	○ ○
3.	Do not <u>break</u> the glass, please.	_____	○ ○
4.	The cat was <u>thein</u> because it did not eat.	_____	○ ○
5.	<u>Which</u> way did you go?	_____	○ ○
6.	Let's all <u>keap</u> together when we go.	_____	○ ○
7.	I want my hair to grow very <u>long</u>.	_____	○ ○
8.	I hit the fence with my <u>stick</u>.	_____	○ ○
9.	My dad has a large dump <u>truke</u>.	_____	○ ○
10.	You do not <u>beleve</u> that I can run fast.	_____	○ ○
11.	Let's run and <u>plae</u>.	_____	○ ○
12.	We can use dirt to fill in the <u>crack</u>.	_____	○ ○

Reading—Context Clues

Read the story, and fill in the blanks using words from the list.

cockatoos	zoo	you	spray	copy	jump
monkeys	colourful	lions	zoo	down	

When you go to the _____, you watch the animals, and they watch you. The elephants may _____ you with water. The _____ swing by their tails. They try to do what you do. Scratch your head, and they will _____ you and do it, too. Jump up and _____, and they will _____, too. My favourite animals at the zoo are the _____. My favourite birds are the _____. They are bright and _____. I love to go to the _____! Don't _____?

Reading—Classification

Write titles for the following lists.

EXAMPLE:

---- **B**irds ----

robin	needle	soap	milk
wren	thread	water	soda
blue jay	scissors	facecloth	water
canary	thimble	towel	juice

whale	lions	ice	mother
shark	tigers	snow	father
dolphin	bears	frost	sister
minnow	elephants	snowman	brother

Mathematics—Metric Measurement

One metre is 100 centimetres. Circle what you think is the best answer.

EXAMPLE:

Is a real tree
(greater than one metre)
or less than one metre?

1. Are you
taller than one metre
or shorter than one metre?

2. Is a real puppy
longer than one metre
or shorter than one metre?

3. Is your bedroom door
taller than one metre
or shorter than one metre?

4. Is the pencil or pen that you are using
longer than one metre
or shorter than one metre?

5. Is this line

greater than one metre
or less than one metre?

Word Study—Contractions

Write the two words that make up the contractions.

1. hasn't _____

2. you'll _____

3. we've _____

4. you're _____

5. isn't _____

6. doesn't _____

7. I'm _____

8. wouldn't _____

9. let's _____

10. she's _____

11. won't _____

12. you've _____

Reading

This passage does not make sense. Mark out all of the qs in each sentence. Then, go back and read the story.

Gregqhadqaqbirthday.qHeqwantedqtoqinviteqallqofqhisq friendsqtoqhisqhouse.qHeqthoughtqthatqitqwouldqbeqfunqtoq haveqeveryoneqbringqtheirqswimmingqsuits.qTheyqcould qrunqthroughqtheqsprinklersqandqswimqinqhisqneighbour's qswimmingqpool.qHeqplannedqonqhavingqaqpizzaqandqiceq cream.qEveryoneqcameqforqtheqparty.qTheyqateqandqswam. qTheyqlaughedqandqyelled.qTheyqplayedqgamesqandqwatch-edqvideosq.Everyoneqhadqaqsuperqtime.qGregalmostqforgotqto qopenqhisqpresentsqbecauseqthereqwasqsoqmuchqtoq do!qHeqtoldqhisqmomqthatqmaybeqnextqyearqtheyqcould qhaveqhisqbirthdayqpartyqforqtwoqdaysqinsteadqofqone.

Language—Creative Writing

It is your birthday. Blow out your candles and make a wish! Write about your wish and/or draw a picture about it.

Follow the directions.

EXAMPLE:

Circle the numerals that are in the <u>tens</u> place. 5③6 ⑧4 1 6⓪2	1.	Circle the numerals that are in the <u>ones</u> place. 26 842 163 924 19 846
2.	Circle the numerals that are in the <u>hundreds</u> place. 481 643 970 1 294 1 122	3. Circle the numerals that are in the <u>tens</u> place. 816 121 6 211 44 729 4 864
4.	What does the circled numeral mean? 51⑥ 6 ones 6 hundreds 6 tens	5. What does the circled numeral mean? ②65 2 ones 2 tens 2 hundreds
6.	What does the circled numeral mean? 2⓪1 0 ones 0 hundreds 0 tens	7. What does the circled numeral mean? 29④ 4 hundreds 4 ones 4 tens

EXAMPLE: Tell how many. 100 100 10 10 1 **221**	8.	**707** ____ tens ____ hundreds ____ ones
9. Tell how many. 100 100 10 10 1 1 _____	10.	**846** ____ tens ____ hundreds ____ ones
11. Tell how many. 100 100 10 10 10 1 _____	12.	**301** ____ tens ____ hundreds ____ ones

Word Study—Alphabetical Order

Put the words in alphabetical order so that the sentences make sense. Write the sentences. Be sure to put an uppercase letter on the first word.

EXAMPLE:

1. talk did she with you? _____ **Did she talk with you?** _____
2. I notebook there left my. _____
3. babies walkers cute in are? _____
4. wildflowers the Allie smelled. _____
5. turtles sneaky I love. _____
6. player zip runs baseball a with. _____
   _____
7. drink do milk dragons? _____
8. water careful in be the. _____

Reading—Recalling Events; Drawing Conclusions

Read the story and answer the questions.

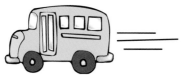

Lori got up late today, so she missed the bus. She had to walk to school. She was tired and cranky when she got there. She promised herself that she would never sleep late again.

1. Why was Lori late for school?

_____

_____

2. Why did she have to walk?

_____

_____

3. What advice do you have for Lori?

_____

_____

Reading—Sequence Sentences in the Correct Order

Let's make a sandwich. Number the steps in the correct order.

_____   Put whatever else you like on your sandwich.

___1___   Take two pieces of bread. Put butter on top of each.

_____   Put the two pieces of bread together.

_____   Next put on the meat and cheese.

_____   Eat your sandwich—yum, yum!

_____   Cut the sandwich in two and put it on a plate.

_____   Clean up after yourself.

Mathematics—Comparing Amounts Using Signs

Write the signs for greater than (>), less than (<), or equal to (=) in the circles.

EXAMPLE:

386 ⊘ 367	474 ◯ 447	184 ◯ 284
254 ◯ 245	442 ◯ 542	898 ◯ 889
780 ◯ 870	501 ◯ 710	999 ◯ 1 000

◯

◯

9 tens ◯ 10 fives	3 fives ◯ 2 tens	25 ones ◯ 4 tens
10 tens ◯ 8 fives	4 tens ◯ 18 ones	8 tens ◯ 12 fives
14 fives ◯ 10 tens	1 hundred ◯ 6 tens	3 hundreds ◯ 20 tens

Phonics—Vowels That You Can See and Hear

Read the words. Write how many vowels you see, and then, write how many vowel sounds you hear.

	vowels	vowel sounds		vowels	vowel sounds
bake	____	____	heard	____	____
puzzle	____	____	radio	____	____
possible	____	____	candy	____	____
cookies	____	____	sneeze	____	____
alphabet	____	____	wanted	____	____
games	____	____	heart	____	____
jump	____	____	useful	____	____
pilot	____	____	beautiful	____	____
fantastic	____	____	wonderful	____	____

Day 8

Word Study—Antonyms

Antonyms are opposites. Read the sentences.
Circle the word that will complete the sentence.

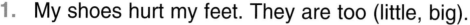

1. My shoes hurt my feet. They are too (little, big).
2. Be sure to (blame, praise) your friends when they do good work.
3. If you do not go now, I will not (allow, refuse) you to go again.
4. Mother told me to wear (dirty, clean) clothes to the party.
5. Troy knows how to take charge of the group. He is a very good (follower, leader).
6. When the light is red, you must remember to (go, stop).
7. The library is a place where we need to be (noisy, quiet).
8. The (sour, sweet) pickle made my mouth feel strange.
9. The bread was so old, it became (fresh, stale).
10. While I am gone, would you please (answer, question) the phone?

Reading—Following Written Directions

Toucan   **Puffin**   **Kingfisher**

1. Colour the kingfisher's head and wings blue-green. Colour his breast red-orange. Leave his throat white. Colour his bill yellow-orange. Draw a post for him to stand on.
2. Colour the toucan's bill any three colours you wish. Colour his throat and breast orange. Colour around his eye green. Colour the rest of him black. Draw a branch for him to sit on.
3. Colour the puffin's bill green, red, and yellow. Leave his head and breast white. Colour the rest of him black, but not too dark. Draw some ice under the puffin's feet.
4. Colour all of the birds' feet orange.

Mathematics—Three-Digit Addition and Subtraction

Add or subtract.

573	832	153	637	638	721
− 132	+ 23	+ 210	− 224	− 532	+ 112

35	263	508	337	544	206
− 25	+ 13	− 305	+ 231	− 234	+ 392

972	684	912	400	805	978
− 421	− 182	+ 87	+ 500	− 202	− 326

Language—Writing Sentences; Capitalization; Punctuation

Find the hidden sentences and write them on the lines. Remember to use uppercase letters and periods.

1.
I	C
L	A
I	N
K	D
E	Y

2.
D	A	N	I
U	R	N	M
C	E	Y	A
K	F	A	L
S	U	N	S

3.
P	N	H	I	A	M	S	O
L	G	M	E	N	I	A	F
A	W	Y	N	D	L	L	F
Y	I	F	D	F	Y	O	U
I	T	R	S	A	I	T	N

1. _____

_____

2. _____

_____

3. _____

_____

Reading—Drawing Conclusions

Read the sentences, and decide whether they are real or make-believe.

Bricks

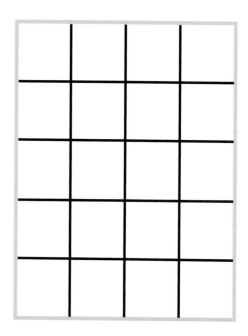

1. Bricks come in different colours. Some are red, yellow, grey, or white. People used to have only red brick houses. Now people use other colours, too.

   | real | make-believe |

3. People can make walls and fences out of bricks. Brick walls and fences are very strong. They seldom break or crumble.

   | real | make-believe |

2. The oldest little pig made his house of bricks to keep out the big, bad wolf. He locked the door and was safe. He lived happily ever after.

   | real | make-believe |

Mathematics—Using a Grid

Copy the picture onto the blank grid.

Mathematics—Multiplication
Match and multiply.

EXAMPLE:

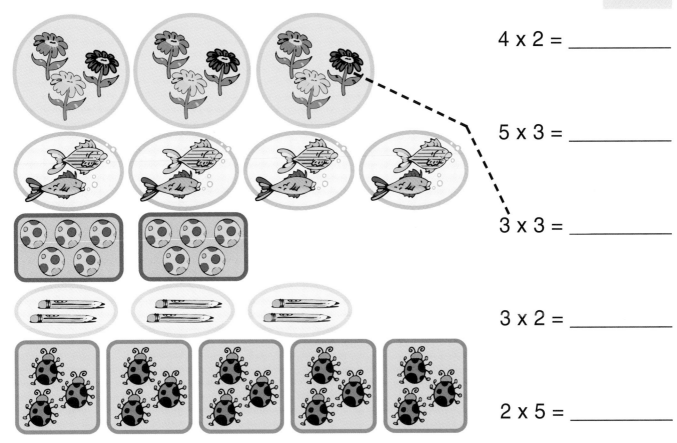

4 x 2 = _____

5 x 3 = _____

3 x 3 = _____

3 x 2 = _____

2 x 5 = _____

Word Study—Spelling
Here is a list of spelling words. Fill in the missing letters, and then, spell the words without the help of an adult.

EXAMPLE:

1. caug **h** t
2. stra__
3. thro__
4. fo__nd
5. wh__le
6. spo__l
7. sh__ll
8. scho__l

9. yo__r
10. sh__uld
11. sho__t
12. doct__r
13. yo__ng
14. sh__re
15. mar__h
16. pret__y

17. f__rst
18. th__rsty
19. m__ddy
20. kn__w
21. kn__w
22. wr__te
23. wr__te
24. gre__t

Reading—Evaluating

If the answer to the question is *yes*, colour the space green.
If the answer is *no*, colour the space purple. Colour the other
spaces yellow.

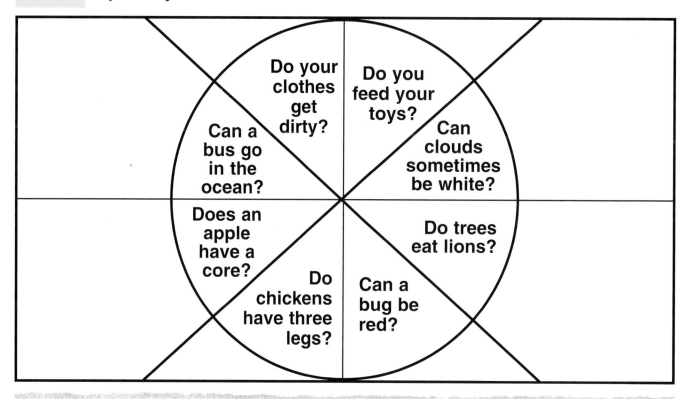

Reading—Recalling Details

In the quiet room, Matt heard the wind howling outside
and the ringing of the telephone inside. He heard his
mother and father talking softly. His sister was singing
to their baby brother, who was crying in his crib. The fish
in the fish tank were gurgling to one another as the dog
barked for something to eat. Matt decided that he can
hear a lot of interesting things if he just listens.

Write down all of the *sound* words in Matt's story.

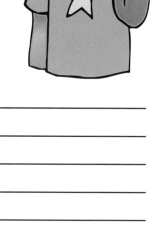

_____

_____

_____

_____

_____

_____

Colour the items in each box to match the fraction.

EXAMPLE:

Colour one-third.  $\dfrac{1}{3}$	Colour two-fourths. 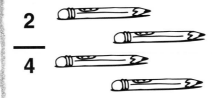 $\dfrac{2}{4}$	Colour three-sixths.  $\dfrac{3}{6}$
Colour seven-tenths.  $\dfrac{7}{10}$	Colour one-fourth. 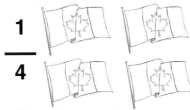 $\dfrac{1}{4}$	Colour five-eighths.  $\dfrac{5}{8}$
Colour three-sevenths.  $\dfrac{3}{7}$	Colour one-half.  $\dfrac{1}{2}$	Colour two-thirds. $\dfrac{2}{3}$

Phonics—Using "Qu" Words

Read the following sentences, and use the *qu-* words to fill in the blanks.

1. The little pigs like to _____.
2. _____ the oranges to make juice.
3. I have a colourful _____ on my bed.
4. Shh! Be very _____.
5. Two dimes and a nickel make a _____.
6. The king and _____ sit on thrones.
7. The door has a _____.
8. A _____ has four corners.
9. I would like to ask a _____.
10. Tests are a type of _____.

question
queen
quiet
quarter
squeal
squeak
square
quiz
quilt
squeeze

Language—Completing Sentences
Finish the "I could . . ." sentences.

1. I could fish if I had a _____.
2. I could write if I had a _____.
3. I could play if I had a _____.
4. I could swim if I had a _____.
5. I could jump if I had a _____.
6. I could eat if I had a _____.
7. I could read if I had a _____.
8. I could colour if I had a _____.

Reading—Classifying Information
Circle *yes* if the sentence is true. Circle *no* if the sentence is false.

1.	Some bears live where it is cold all year.	yes	no
2.	You can see through a door.	yes	no
3.	Ants live in communities.	yes	no
4.	We go to the theatre to go swimming.	yes	no
5.	To exchange something means you keep it.	yes	no
6.	We celebrate on Canada Day.	yes	no
7.	Horses wear moccasins.	yes	no
8.	Elevators go from side to side.	yes	no
9.	A house is built on a foundation.	yes	no
10.	Conductors are people who work on automobiles.	yes	no
11.	A wrench is a tool.	yes	no
12.	A tadpole turns into a frog.	yes	no

Mathematics—Evaluating Answers to Questions

Pretend you are the teacher. Correct this paper with a red pencil. __X__ wrong __C__ correct.

Day
12

EXAMPLE:

423	784	434	324	38	522
+ 138	− 107	+ 128	+ 267	+ 19	+ 139
561 C	618 X	562	592	57	760

667	410	948	546	634	315
− 419	− 125	− 819	− 317	− 571	− 142
247	305	129	218	63	173

342	467	861	933	429	193
− 237	+ 161	− 671	− 673	+ 364	+ 184
105	628	210	260	893	377

Phonics—Recognizing Long, Short, and Silent Vowel Sounds

Mark the vowels: ⌣short   —long   silent /

1. hōlȩ
2. cŭt
3. meat
4. use
5. children
6. gave
7. which
8. get
9. pipe
10. invite

11. tube
12. music
13. fly
14. catch
15. goat
16. table
17. visit
18. these
19. glad
20. find

21. best
22. plant
23. read
24. railroad
25. leave
26. mop
27. think
28. clock
29. smile
30. much

Reading—Main Idea

Read the following story, and then, underline the sentence that tells what the story is about.

All birds are alike in some ways and different in others. They all have wings, but not all of them fly. Some are tame, and some are wild. Some birds sing. Some talk. Some are gentle; others are not so gentle. Some fly very high and far; others do not. Some birds are colourful, while others are quite drab.

- Some birds are tame, others are not.
- All birds are strange and colourful.
- Birds are alike and different from each other.

Mathematics—Using a Dotted Grid to Make Shapes

How many designs with dots can you make? Try to use every dot.

EXAMPLE:

Mathematics—Problem Solving
Read and answer each problem.

EXAMPLE:

There are 3 cages, with 2 rabbits in each cage. How many rabbits are there in all?

__3__ x __2__ = | 6 | rabbits

1. Allie has 3 vases with 4 flowers in each vase. How many flowers does she have in all?

____ x ____ = ☐ flowers

2. Denise has 4 packages of gum with 5 pieces in each package. How many pieces does she have?

____ x ____ = ☐ pieces

3. Dad has 3 glasses. He put 2 straws in each glass. How many straws did Dad put in the glasses?

____ x ____ = ☐ straws

4. Mother made 3 shirts. She put 3 buttons on each shirt. How many buttons did Mother use?

____ x ____ = ☐ buttons

5. We have 4 tables for the party. Each table needs 4 chairs. How many chairs do we need in all?

____ x ____ = ☐ chairs

Word Study—Understanding Words with More Than One Meaning
Match the words with the correct meanings.

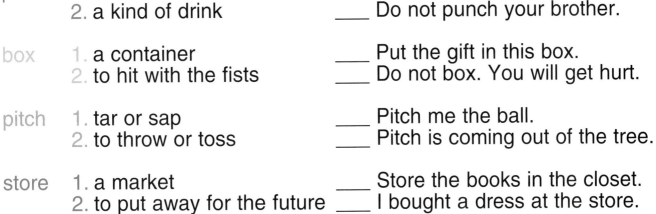

fly   1. a small insect   __2__ The birds can fly.
        2. to move through the air   __1__ The spider ate the fly.

punch 1. to hit someone   ____ I drank some orange punch.
        2. a kind of drink   ____ Do not punch your brother.

box   1. a container   ____ Put the gift in this box.
        2. to hit with the fists   ____ Do not box. You will get hurt.

pitch 1. tar or sap   ____ Pitch me the ball.
        2. to throw or toss   ____ Pitch is coming out of the tree.

store 1. a market   ____ Store the books in the closet.
        2. to put away for the future ____ I bought a dress at the store.

well   1. healthy, not sick   ____ Drop a penny in the well.
        2. a hole to collect water ____ Are you feeling well?

Reading—Noting Details

Connect the sentences with the correct word from the box.

EXAMPLE:

1. This lets you talk to someone far away.
2. This is something you can walk through when you are home.
3. This is the opposite of <u>back</u>.
4. This is what you might do when you are sad.
5. This is something that is found all around you.
6. This is your mom or dad's sister.
7. When something itches, you usually do this.

Word List

scratch

cry

phone

front

door

air

aunt

Language—Alliteration

Writing a sentence where all the words start with the same letter can be fun. Try your skills with each letter.

EXAMPLE: **Freddy farmer fixes flats.**

1. **C**

_____

2. **I**

_____

3. **S**

_____

4. **T**

_____

5. **R**

_____

Mathematics—Multiplication Facts

Multiply.

1. 5 x 1 = _____   **2.** 5 x 5 = _____   **3.** 2 x 3 = _____

1 x 0 = _____   2 x 2 = _____   3 x 4 = _____

4 x 2 = _____   3 x 3 = _____   4 x 5 = _____

0 x 1 = _____   1 x 1 = _____   2 x 5 = _____

3 x 5 = _____   4 x 1 = _____   1 x 2 = _____

4.
3	4	3	6	7	2	5	4
x 5	x 5	x 4	x 2	x 1	x 3	x 5	x 0

5.   2 x 4 = _____   1 x 3 = _____   5 x 3 = _____

5 x 6 = _____   2 x 6 = _____   0 x 5 = _____

Word Study—Recognizing Syllables

Remember, there are as many syllables in a word as there are vowel sounds. Write how many vowels, vowel sounds, and syllables are in each word.

△ = number of vowels   □ = number of syllables   ○ = number of vowel sounds

EXAMPLE:

goat   ② |1| ①   uncle   △ □ ○

potato   △ □ ○   mailbox   △ □ ○

racoon   △ □ ○   dentist   △ □ ○

giant   △ □ ○   tree   △ □ ○

umbrella △ □ ○   racquetball △ □ ○

cupcake △ □ ○   sandbox   △ □ ○

watermelon △ □ ○   railroad   △ □ ○

Day 14

Reading—Noting Details

Read each sentence. Write the correct answer.

1. Sam is going to Paul's football game.
   Who is going to the game? _____
   Whose game is it? _____

2. Susan is taking care of Joyce's baby.
   To whom does the baby belong? _____
   Who is taking care of the baby? _____

3. He is singing the teacher's favourite song.
   Whose favourite song is he singing? _____
   Who is singing? _____

4. Al is reading Sam's books.
   To whom do the books belong? _____
   Who is reading? _____

Language—Brainstorming Descriptive Words

Write words on each sun that tell something you are doing or would like to do in the summer.

Mathematics—Three-Digit Addition and Subtraction

Add or subtract.

462	483	746	762	821	563
+ 128	− 280	+ 222	+ 29	− 530	− 125

236	924	233	407	852	365
+ 171	− 360	− 114	− 304	− 539	+ 171

$3.42	$6.29	$8.32	$3.73	$1.78	$5.32
− 2.11	+ 2.11	− 7.19	+ 0.53	+ 2.15	− 1.91

Mathematics—Interpreting a Line Graph

Use the line graph to answer the questions.

Wendy works in a bakery. Every day she makes bread.

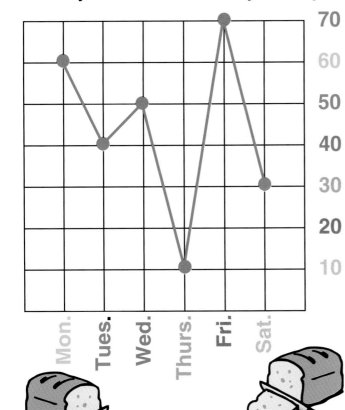

1. How many loaves of bread did Wendy bake on Saturday?

   _____

2. On which two days did Wendy bake 100 loaves of bread altogether? _____ and _____

3. On which day did Wendy bake the most loaves?

   _____

4. On which day did Wendy bake the least? _____

5. Name two other days that Wendy baked 100 loaves of bread: _____ and

   _____

Reading—Recalling Details

Read the poem, and then, do the activity below.

My Shadow

I have a little shadow that goes in and out with me,
And what can be the use of him is more than I can see.
He is very, very like me from the heels up to the head;
And I see him jump before me, when I jump into bed.
—Robert Louis Stevenson

1. What does your shadow do when you jump into bed?

_____

_____

2. Who does your shadow look like?

_____

_____

3. When do you see your shadow?

_____

_____

4. What else can your shadow do besides jump?

_____

_____

Language—Recognizing Complete and Incomplete Sentences

Write *yes* if the sentence is complete or *no* if it is not complete.

EXAMPLE:
A. Inside a large. **No**
B. Someone is walking on the sidewalk. **Yes**

1. Ted helped Jane. _____
2. That road goes to. _____
3. I went to a movie last night. _____
4. We played in the park by. _____
5. Who is going to? _____
6. Today is my birthday. _____
7. Under the swing in front of the house. _____
8. Every Friday after school. _____
9. Did you enjoy reading that book? _____
10. Andy likes to play football. _____

Words to Sound, Read, and Spell

spring	tape	together	valley
squirrel	taste	told	vegetable
stack	teach	tomorrow	very
stair	teacher	tonight	village
stand	team	too	visit
star	tell	took	voice
stare	temper	tooth	wagon
start	ten	touch	wait
stay	test	toward	wake
stick	thank	towel	walk
still	that	town	wall
stone	the	toy	want
stood	their	track	warm
store	them	trade	warn
storm	then	trail	was
story	there	train	wash
straight	these	trap	waste
strange	they	travel	watch
stream	thin	tree	water
street	thing	trip	wave
strength	think	trouble	way
string	third	truck	wear
strong	this	true	weather
stuck	those	try	weave
study	though	tunnel	week
such	thought	turn	weigh
sudden	thousand	turtle	welcome
summer	three	twenty	well
sun	threw	twist	went
supper	through	two	were
suppose	throw	ugly	west
sure	ticket	uncle	wet
surprise	tie	under	whale
swim	tight	understand	what
table	time	until	wheat
tail	tiny	up	wheel
take	tire	us	when
talk	title	use	where
tall	today	usually	which

Words to Sound, Read, and Spell

while	wing	work	yesterday
whisper	winter	world	yet
whistle	wipe	worm	you
white	wire	would	young
who	wish	wrinkle	your
whole	with	write	yourself
why	woke	written	
wide	woman	wrong	
wife	wonder	wrote	
will	wonderful	yard	
win	won't	year	
wind	wood	yellow	
window	word	yes	

Answer Pages

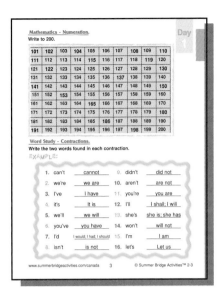

Section 1

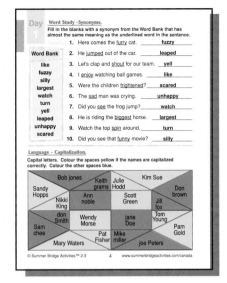

Page 3

Page 3

Page 4

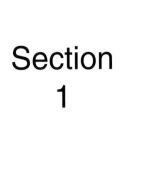

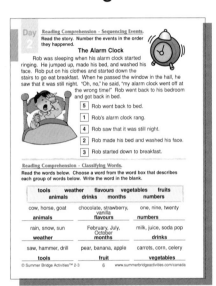

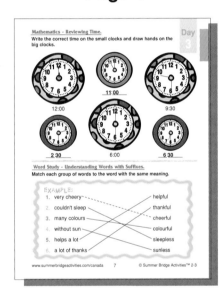

Page 5

Page 6

Page 7

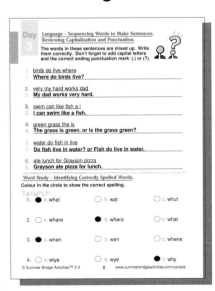

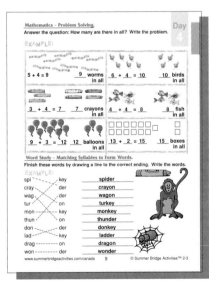

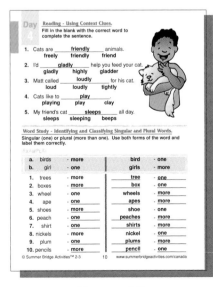

Page 8

Page 9

Page 10

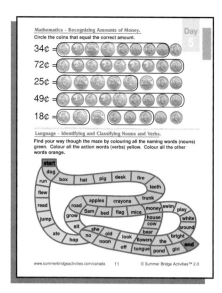

Page 11

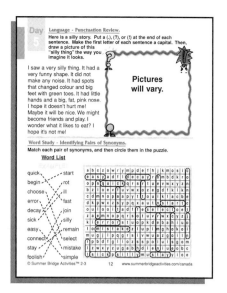

Page 12

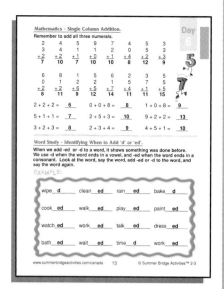

Page 13

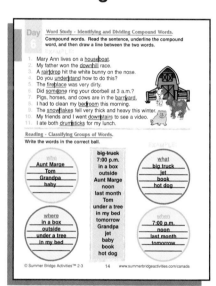

Page 14

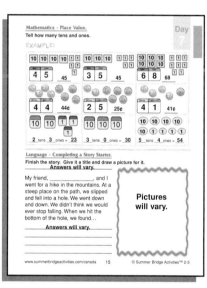

Page 15

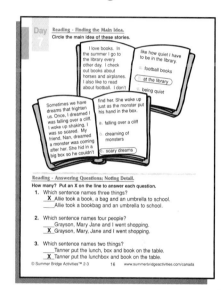

Page 16

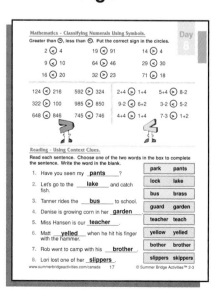

Page 17

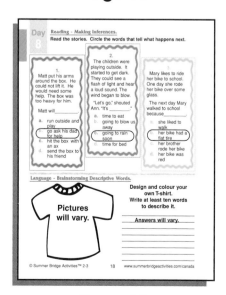

Page 18

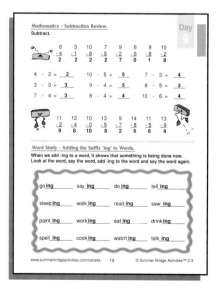

Page 19

Page 20

Day 9

Reading - Answering General Questions with Sentences.

Answer the questions. Write complete sentences.

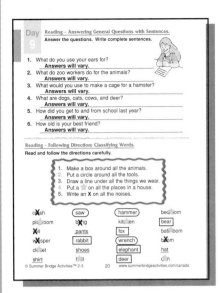

1. What do you use your ears for? **Answers will vary.**
2. What do zoo workers do for the animals? **Answers will vary.**
3. What would you use to make a cage for a hamster? **Answers will vary.**
4. What are dogs, cats, cows, and deer? **Answers will vary.**
5. How did you get to and from school last year? **Answers will vary.**
6. How old is your best friend? **Answers will vary.**

Reading - Following Direction; Classifying Words.

Read and follow the directions carefully.

1. Make a box around all the animals.
2. Put a circle around all the tools.
3. Draw a line under all the things we wear.
4. Put a ☆ on all the places in a house.
5. Write an **X** on all the noises.

crash (X)	(saw)	(hammer)	bedroom ☆
playroom ☆	bang (X)	kitchen ☆	[bear]
yell (X)	<u>pants</u>	[fox]	bathroom ☆
whisper (X)	[rabbit]	(wrench)	boom (X)
closet ☆	<u>shoes</u>	[elephant]	<u>hat</u>
<u>shirt</u>	hall ☆	[deer]	den ☆

Page 21

Day 10

Mathematics - Subtraction.

Subtract 6	
8	2
12	6
9	3
11	5
7	1
13	7

Subtract 8	
8	0
11	3
12	4
19	11
10	2
14	6

Subtract 7	
14	7
8	1
7	0
10	3
12	5
9	2

Geography - Using a Mapping Key to Locate Information.

Look at the map and map key to answer the questions.

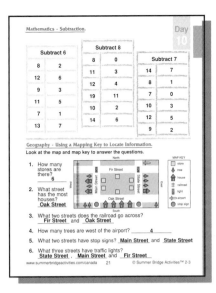

1. How many stores are there? **6**
2. What street has the most houses? **Oak Street**
3. What two streets does the railroad go across? **Fir Street** and **Oak Street**
4. How many trees are west of the airport? **4**
5. What two streets have stop signs? **Main Street** and **State Street**
6. What three streets have traffic lights? **State Street**, **Main Street** and **Fir Street**

Page 22

Day 10

Reading - Using Words Ending with 'ion' in Sentences.

Fill in the blanks. Use words from the box.

vacation, station, sections, nation, addition, mention, collection, lotion, transportation, fraction, question, protection

1. This orange has ten **sections** in it.
2. A car is one kind of **transportation**.
3. Can you answer my **question**?
4. We went on a **vacation** to Hawaii.
5. My brother and I have a stamp **collection**.
6. I like to do hard **addition** problems.
7. The train stops at every **station**.
8. We needed some **protection** from the wind.
9. Is Japan a big **nation**?
10. Linda put some **lotion** on her hands.
11. Is one-half a **fraction**?
12. Don't **mention** this secret to Donald.

Reading - Using Number Words.

Fill in the boxes with number words. Use some words more than once.

EXAMPLE: **Answers may vary.**

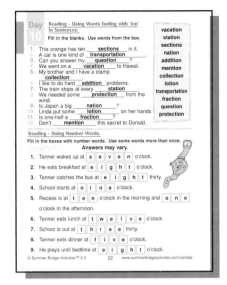

1. Tanner wakes up at s e v e n o'clock.
2. He eats breakfast at e i g h t o'clock.
3. Tanner catches the bus at e i g h t thirty.
4. School starts at n i n e o'clock.
5. Recess is at t e n o'clock in the morning and o n e o'clock in the afternoon.
6. Tanner eats lunch at t w e l v e o'clock.
7. School is out at t h r e e thirty.
8. Tanner eats dinner at f i v e o'clock.
9. He plays until bedtime at e i g h t o'clock.

Page 23

Day 11

Mathematics - Identifying Number Words.

Write the numeral on the line beside each number.

forty	40	eight	8	one	1
sixteen	16	seventeen	17	eighteen	18
four	4	fifty	50	thirty	30
nine	9	two	2	ninety-nine	99
twelve	12	nineteen	19	seven	7
ten	10	eleven	11	thirteen	13
fifteen	15	thirty-three	33	fourteen	14
twenty	20	five	5	six	6

Word Study - Rhyming Words.

Write five words that rhyme with each key word.

EXAMPLE: sack — back

rock, deck, lick, truck, queen, king, song, rung, jump

Answers will vary.

Page 24

Day 11

Language - Recognizing the Meaning of Pronouns.

Tell what or who the underlined words mean.

EXAMPLE: The boys ran away. <u>They</u> ran to school. They = **boys**

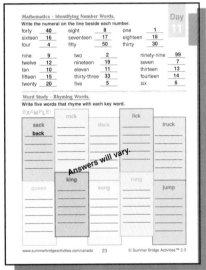

1. Carla and I like horses. We ride <u>them</u> every day. them = **horses**
2. Grandma called today. <u>She</u> is coming to see us. She = **Grandma**
3. Joe would like to fly in a jet. <u>He</u> has never been in <u>one</u>. He = **Joe** one = **jet**
4. This summer, I am at camp. I like it <u>here</u>. here = **camp**
5. I lost my best umbrella. <u>It</u> is blue. It = **umbrella**
6. Lee has two dogs. <u>They</u> are both black. They = **dogs**
7. Ted and I are late for the movie. John is waiting for <u>us</u>. us = **Ted and I**
8. I left a note for Mom. <u>It</u> tells <u>her</u> where I am. It = **note** her = **Mom**

Word Study - Identifying Correctly Spelled Words.

Read each sentence. Look carefully at the underlined word. Is it spelled right or wrong? Mark your answer.

	Right	Wrong
1. Randy <u>ate</u> toast with jam on it.	●	○
2. We <u>wunt</u> to the store for some candy.	○	●
3. The dog will <u>hund</u> for his bone.	○	●
4. We will <u>plant</u> our garden tonight.	●	○
5. The <u>keng</u> asked the queen to come quick.	○	●
6. This is the <u>ent</u> of my story.	○	●
7. I want my hair to grow very <u>long</u>.	●	○
8. <u>Think</u> of a good name for a pet.	●	○
9. Do you like to <u>sing</u> with friends?	●	○
10. Don't let the cat <u>lant</u> on my bed.	○	●

Page 25

Day 12

Mathematics - Place Value.

What does the circled digit mean? Circle the answer. Be sure to read the words.

EXAMPLE: 89 — 9 tens / **(9 ones)**

Number	Answer
29	**(2 tens)** / 2 ones
14	**(1 ten)** / 2 ones
63	**(3 ones)** / 3 tens
38	**(3 tens)** / 3 ones
10	0 tens / **(0 ones)**
4	4 tens / **(4 ones)**
71	7 ones / **(7 tens)**
42	**(4 tens)** / 4 ones
99	**(9 ones)** / 9 tens
56	**(5 tens)** / 5 ones
60	**(0 ones)** / 0 tens

Language - Capitalization in Titles.

Story Titles. Rule: The first and all other important words in a story or book title begin with a capital letter. Write these story titles correctly.

EXAMPLE:

1. an exciting camping trip — **An Exciting Camping Trip**
2. my ride on an elephant — **My Ride on an Elephant**
3. the day we missed school — **The Day We Missed School**
4. pets are fun — **Pets are Fun**
5. a real fire drill — **A Real Fire Drill**
6. my vacation this summer — **My Vacation This Summer**
7. a lost puppy — **A Lost Puppy**
8. walking in the rain — **Walking in the Rain**

Page 26

Day 12

Mathematics - Graphing: Interpretations.

Study the pictograph. Read the questions and circle your answer. The first one is done for you.

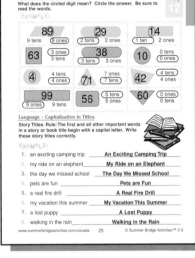

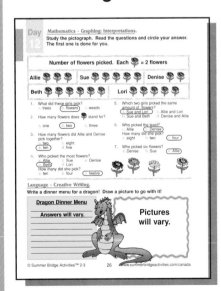

Number of flowers picked. Each ✿ = 2 flowers

Allie	✿✿✿
Sue	✿✿✿✿✿
Denise	✿✿
Beth	✿✿✿✿✿✿
Lori	✿✿✿✿✿

1. What did these girls pick? a. trees **(b. flowers)** c. weeds
2. How many flowers does ✿ stand for? a. one **(b. two)** c. three
3. How many flowers did Allie and Denise pick together? a. two **(b. ten)** c. eight d. five
4. Who picked the most flowers? a. Allie **(b. Beth)** c. Sue d. Lori e. Denise. How many did she pick? a. ten b. four **(c. twelve)**
5. Which two girls picked the same amount of flowers? **(a. Sue and Lori)** b. Sue and Beth c. Allie and Lori d. Denise and Allie
6. Who picked the least? a. Allie **(b. Denise)**. How many did she pick? a. eight b. two **(c. four)**
7. Who picked six flowers? a. Denise b. Sue **(c. Allie)**

Language - Creative Writing.

Write a dinner menu for a dragon! Draw a picture to go with it!

Dragon Dinner Menu

Answers will vary.

Pictures will vary.

Page 27

Day 13

Mathematics - Problem Solving.

Read the story. Write the problem and the answer.

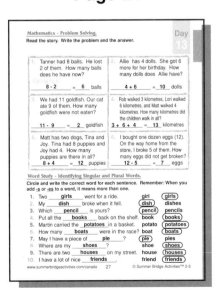

1. Tanner had 8 balls. He lost 2 of them. How many balls does he have now? **8 - 2 = 6 balls**
2. Allie has 4 dolls. She got 6 more for her birthday. How many dolls does Allie have? **4 + 6 = 10 dolls**
3. We had 11 goldfish. Our cat ate 9 of them. How many goldfish were not eaten? **11 - 9 = 2 goldfish**
4. Rob walked 3 kilometres, Lori walked 6 kilometres, and Matt walked 4 kilometres. How many kilometres did the children walk in all? **3 + 6 + 4 = 13 kilometres**
5. Matt has two dogs, Tina and Joy. Tina had 8 puppies and Joy had 4. How many puppies are there in all? **8 + 4 = 12 puppies**
6. I bought one dozen eggs (12). On the way home from the store, I broke 5 of them. How many eggs did not get broken? **12 - 5 = 7 eggs**

Word Study - Identifying Singular and Plural Words.

Circle and write the correct word for each sentence. Remember: When you add -s or -es to a word, it means more than one.

1. Two **girls** went for a ride. girl **(girls)**
2. My **dish** broke when it fell. **(dish)** dishes
3. Which **pencil** is yours? **(pencil)** pencils
4. Put all the **books** back on the shelf. book **(books)**
5. Martin carried the **potatoes** in a basket. potato **(potatoes)**
6. How many **boats** were in the race? boat **(boats)**
7. May I have a piece of **pie**? **(pie)** pies
8. Where are my **shoes**? shoe **(shoes)**
9. There are two **houses** on my street. house **(houses)**
10. I have a lot of nice **friends**. friend **(friends)**

Page 28

Day 13

Reading - Identifying Word Meanings.

What does the underlined word mean? Circle your answer.

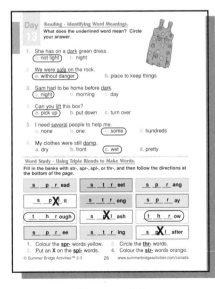

1. She has on a <u>dark</u> green dress. **(a. not light)** b. night
2. We were <u>safe</u> on the rock. **(a. without danger)** b. place to keep things
3. Sam had to be home before <u>dark</u>. **(a. night)** b. morning c. day
4. Can you <u>lift</u> this box? **(a. pick up)** b. put down c. turn over
5. I need <u>several</u> people to help me. a. none b. one **(c. some)** d. hundreds
6. My clothes were still <u>damp</u>. a. dry b. front **(c. wet)** d. pretty

Word Study - Using Triple Blends to Make Words.

Fill in the banks with str-, spr-, spl-, or thr-, and then follow the directions at the bottom of the page.

s p r ead	s t r eet	s p r ang
s p l it (X)	s t r ong	s p r ay
(t h r ough)	s p l ash (X)	(t h r ow)
s p r ee	s t r ing	s p l atter (X)

1. Colour the **spr-** words yellow.
2. Put an X on the **spl-** words.
3. Circle the **thr-** words.
4. Colour the **str-** words orange.

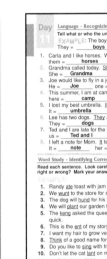

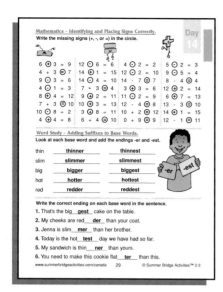

Page 29

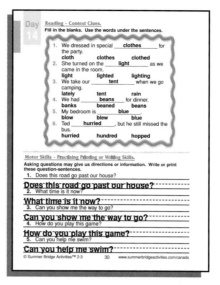

Page 30

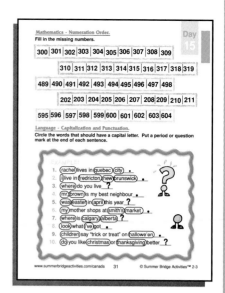

Page 31

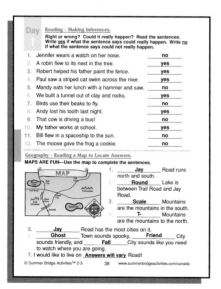

Page 32

Section 2

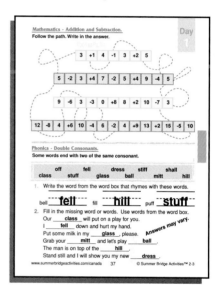

Page 37

Page 38

Page 39

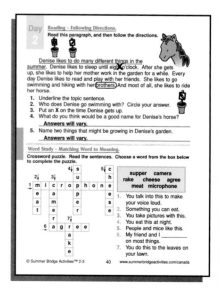

Page 40

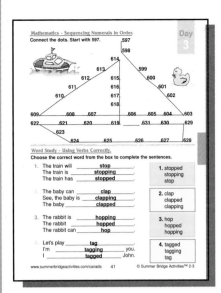

Page 41

Mathematics - Sequencing Numerals in Order.
Connect the dots. Start with 597.

Word Study - Using Verbs Correctly.
Choose the correct word from the box to complete the sentences.

1. The train will ___ **stop**
   The train is ___ **stopping**
   The train has ___ **stopped**

2. The baby can ___ **clap**
   See, the baby is ___ **clapping**
   The baby ___ **clapped**

3. The rabbit is ___ **hopping**
   The rabbit ___ **hopped**
   The rabbit can ___ **hop**

4. Let's play ___ **tag**
   I'm ___ **tagging** ___ you.
   I ___ **tagged** ___ John.

1. stopping
   stopping
   stop

2. clap
   clapped
   clapping

3. hop
   hopped
   hopping

4. tagged
   tagging
   tag

www.summerbridgeactivities.com/canada 41 © Summer Bridge Activities™ 2-3

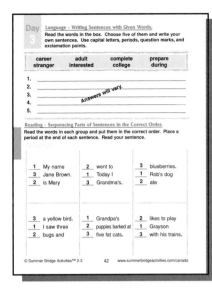

Page 42

Day 3

Language - Writing Sentences with Given Words.
Read the words in the box. Choose five of them and write your own sentences. Use capital letters, periods, question marks, and exclamation points.

| career | adult | complete | prepare |
| stranger | interested | college | during |

1. _____
2. _____
3. _____ Answers will vary.
4. _____
5. _____

Reading - Sequencing Parts of Sentences in the Correct Order.
Read the words in each group and put them in the correct order. Place a period at the end of each sentence. Read your sentence.

1 My name	2 went to	3 blueberries.
3 Jane Brown.	1 Today I	1 Rob's dog
2 is Mary	3 Grandma's.	2 ate

3 a yellow bird.	1 Grandpa's	2 likes to play
1 I saw three	2 puppies barked at	1 Grayson
2 bugs and	3 five fat cats.	3 with his trains.

© Summer Bridge Activities™ 2-3 42 www.summerbridgeactivities.com/canada

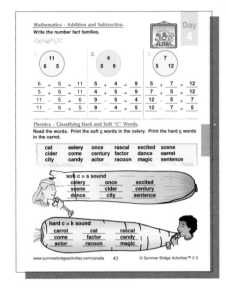

Page 43

Mathematics - Addition and Subtraction.
Write the number fact families.

EXAMPLE:

1. 11 / 6 5
2. 4 / 5 9
3. 7 / 5 12

6 + 5 = 11   5 + 4 = 9   5 + 7 = 12
5 + 6 = 11   4 + 5 = 9   7 + 5 = 12
11 - 5 = 6   9 - 5 = 4   12 - 5 = 7
11 - 6 = 5   9 - 4 = 5   12 - 7 = 5

Phonics - Classifying Hard and Soft "C" Words.
Read the words. Print the soft c words in the celery. Print the hard c words in the carrot.

cat	celery	once	rascal	excited	scene
cider	come	century	factor	dance	carrot
city	candy	actor	racoon	magic	sentence

soft c = s sound
celery   once   excited
scene   cider   century
dance   city   sentence

hard c = k sound
carrot	cat	rascal
come	factor	candy
actor	racoon	magic

www.summerbridgeactivities.com/canada 43 © Summer Bridge Activities™ 2-3

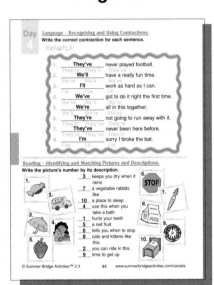

Page 44

Day 4

Language - Recognizing and Using Contractions.
Write the correct contraction for each sentence.

EXAMPLE:

1. **They've** never played football.
2. **We'll** have a really fun time.
3. **I'll** work as hard as I can.
4. **We've** got to do it right the first time.
5. **We're** all in this together.
6. **They're** not going to run away with it.
7. **They've** never been here before.
8. **I'm** sorry I broke the bat.

Reading - Identifying and Matching Pictures and Descriptions.
Write the picture's number by its description.

3 keeps you dry when it rains
7 a vegetable rabbits like
10 a place to sleep
4 use this when you take a bath
1 hurts your teeth
5 a red fruit
6 tells you when to stop
8 cats and kittens like this
2 you can ride in this
9 time to get up

© Summer Bridge Activities™ 2-3 44 www.summerbridgeactivities.com/canada

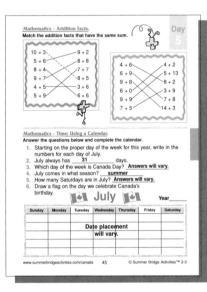

Page 45

Mathematics - Addition Facts.
Match the addition facts that have the same sum.

10 + 3   9 + 2
5 + 6   8 + 8
8 + 4   7 + 7
9 + 7   8 + 5
4 + 5   9 + 9
5 + 9   6 + 6

4 + 6   4 + 2
6 + 9   5 + 13
9 + 8   6 + 9
6 + 0   6 + 9
7 + 5   7 + 8
7 + 5   14 + 3

Mathematics - Time: Using a Calendar.
Answer the questions below and complete the calendar.

1. Starting on the proper day of the week for this year, write in the numbers for each day of July.
2. July always has __31__ days.
3. Which day of the week is Canada Day? Answers will vary.
4. July comes in what season? __summer__
5. How many Saturdays are in July? Answers will vary.
6. Draw a flag on the day we celebrate Canada's birthday.

July   Year ____

Sunday	Monday	Tuesday	Wednesday	Thursday	Friday	Saturday
		Date placement will vary.				

www.summerbridgeactivities.com/canada 45 © Summer Bridge Activities™ 2-3

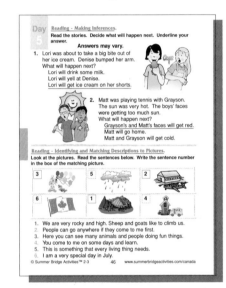

Page 46

Day 5

Reading - Making Inferences.
Read the stories. Decide what will happen next. Underline your answer.

Answers may vary.

1. Lori was about to take a big bite out of her ice cream. Denise bumped her arm. What will happen next?
   Lori will drink some milk.
   Lori will yell at Denise.
   Lori will get ice cream on her shorts.

2. Matt was playing tennis with Grayson. The sun was very hot. The boys' faces were getting too much sun. What will happen next?
   Grayson's and Matt's faces will get red.
   Matt will go home.
   Matt and Grayson will get cold.

Reading - Identifying and Matching Descriptions to Pictures.
Look at the pictures. Read the sentences below. Write the sentence number in the box of the matching picture.

3   5   2
6   1   4

1. We are very rocky and high. Sheep and goats like to climb us.
2. People can go anywhere if they come to me first.
3. Here you can see many animals and people doing fun things.
4. You come to me on some days and learn.
5. This is something that every living thing needs.
6. I am a very special day in July.

© Summer Bridge Activities™ 2-3 46 www.summerbridgeactivities.com/canada

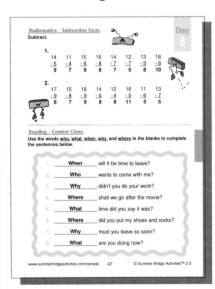

Page 47

Mathematics - Subtraction Facts.
Subtract.

1.
14 11 15 16 14 12 13 18
-5 -4 -6 -8 -7 -7 -5 -8
 9   7   9   8   7   5   8 10

2.
17 15 18 14 12 16 11 13
-9 -8 -9 -6 -4 -5 -6 -7
 8   7   9   8   8 11   5   6

Reading - Context Clues.
Use the words who, what, when, why, and where in the blanks to complete the sentences below.

1. **When** will it be time to leave?
2. **Who** wants to come with me?
3. **Why** didn't you do your work?
4. **Where** shall we go after the movie?
5. **What** time did you say it was?
6. **Where** did you put your shoes and socks?
7. **Why** must you leave so soon?
8. **What** are you doing now?

www.summerbridgeactivities.com/canada 47 © Summer Bridge Activities™ 2-3

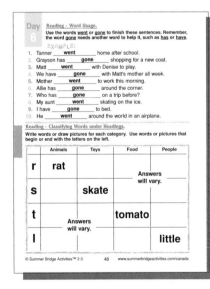

Page 48

Day 6

Reading - Word Usage.
Use the words went or gone to finish these sentences. Remember, the word gone needs another word to help it, such as has or have.

EXAMPLE:

1. Tanner **went** home after school.
2. Grayson has **gone** shopping for a new coat.
3. Matt **went** with Denise to play.
4. We have **gone** with Matt's mother all week.
5. Mother **went** to work this morning.
6. Allie has **gone** around the corner.
7. Who has **gone** on a trip before?
8. My aunt **went** skating on the ice.
9. I have **gone** to bed.
10. He **went** around the world in an airplane.

Reading - Classifying Words under Headings.
Write words or draw pictures for each category. Use words or pictures that begin or end with the letters on the left.

	Animals	Toys	Food	People
r	rat			Answers will vary.
s		skate		
t			tomato	Answers will vary.
l				little

© Summer Bridge Activities™ 2-3 48 www.summerbridgeactivities.com/canada

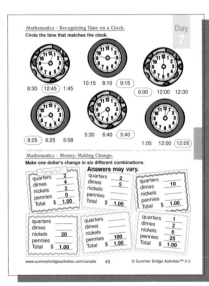

Page 49

Day 7

Mathematics - Recognizing Time on a Clock.
Circle the time that matches the clock.

8:30 (12:45) 1:45
10:15 8:10 (9:15)
(6:00) 12:00 12:30
8:25 6:25 5:08
5:30 6:40 (5:40)
1:05 12:00 (12:05)

Mathematics - Money: Making Change.
Make one dollar's change in six different combinations.

Answers may vary.

quarters	2
dimes	4
nickels	2
pennies	0
Total	$ 1.00

quarters	2
dimes	5
nickels	
pennies	
Total	$ 1.00

quarters	
dimes	10
nickels	
pennies	
Total	$ 1.00

quarters	
dimes	
nickels	20
pennies	
Total	$ 1.00

quarters	
dimes	
nickels	
pennies	100
Total	$ 1.00

quarters	1
dimes	6
nickels	
pennies	25
Total	$ 1.00

www.summerbridgeactivities.com/canada 49 © Summer Bridge Activities™ 2-3

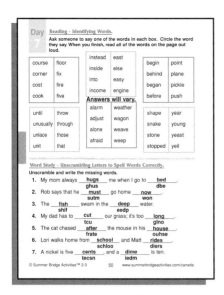

Page 50

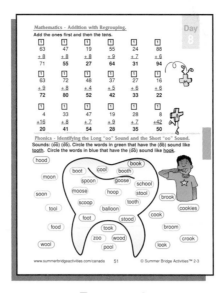

Page 51

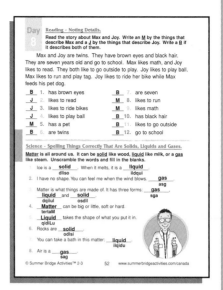

Page 52

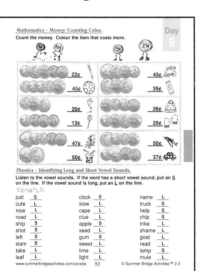

Page 53

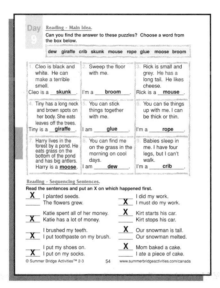

Page 54

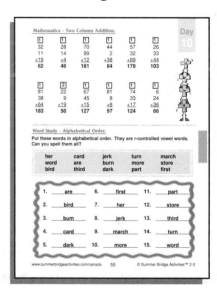

Page 55

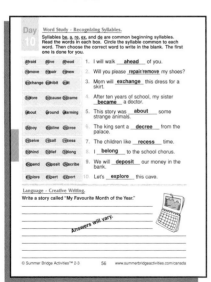

Page 56

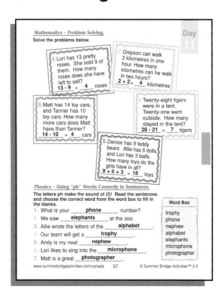

Page 57

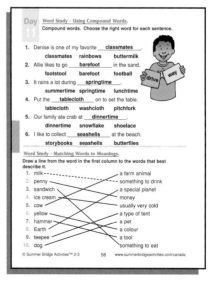

Page 58

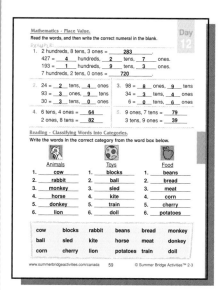

Page 59

Page 60

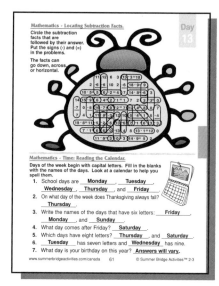

Page 61

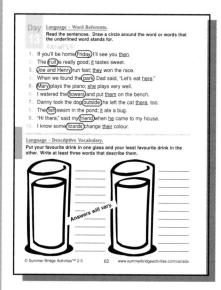

Page 62

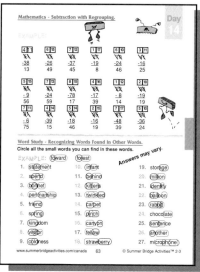

Page 63

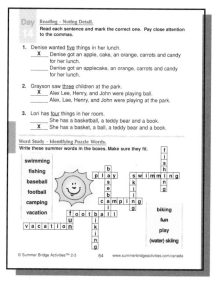

Page 64

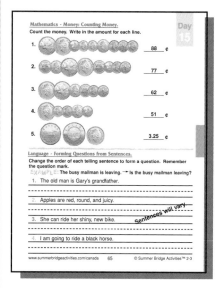

Page 65

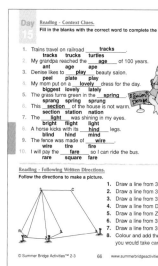

Page 66

Page 67

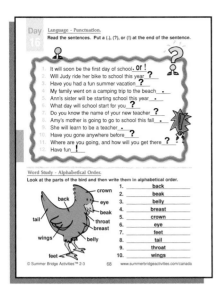

Page 68

Language - Punctuation.
Read the sentences. Put a (.), (?), or (!) at the end of the sentence.

1. It will soon be the first day of school. or !
2. Will Judy ride her bike to school this year ?
3. Have you had a fun summer vacation ?
4. My family went on a camping trip to the beach .
5. Ann's sister will be starting school this year .
6. What day will school start for you ?
7. Do you know the name of your new teacher ?
8. Amy's mother is going to go to school this fall .
9. She will learn to be a teacher .
10. Have you gone anywhere before ?
11. Where are you going, and how will you get there ?
12. Have fun !

Word Study - Alphabetical Order.
Look at the parts of the bird and then write them in alphabetical order.

1. back
2. beak
3. belly
4. breast
5. crown
6. eye
7. feet
8. tail
9. throat
10. wings

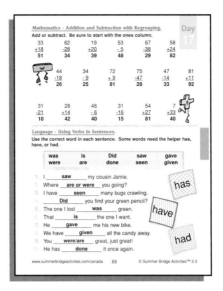

Page 69

Mathematics - Addition and Subtraction with Regrouping.
Add or subtract. Be sure to start with the ones column.

| 33 +18 = 51 | 62 -28 = 34 | 19 +20 = 39 | 53 -5 = 48 | 67 -38 = 29 | 58 +24 = 82 |

| 44 -18 = 26 | 34 -9 = 25 | 72 +9 = 81 | 75 -47 = 28 | 47 -14 = 33 | 81 +11 = 92 |

| 31 -21 = 10 | 28 +14 = 42 | 46 -6 = 40 | 31 -16 = 15 | 54 +27 = 81 | 7 +33 = 40 |

Language - Using Verbs in Sentences.
Use the correct word in each sentence. Some words need the helper has, have, or had.

| was | is | Did | saw | gave |
| were | are | done | seen | given |

1. I __saw__ my cousin Jamie.
2. Where __are or were__ you going?
3. I have __seen__ many bugs crawling.
4. __Did__ you find your green pencil?
5. The one I lost __was__ green.
6. That __is__ the one I want.
7. He __gave__ me his new bike.
8. We have __given__ all the candy away.
9. You __were/are__ great, just great!
10. He has __done__ it once again.

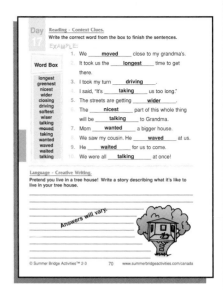

Page 70

Reading - Context Clues.
Write the correct word from the box to finish the sentences.

Word Box: longest, greenest, nicest, wider, closing, driving, softest, wiser, talking, moved, taking, wanted, waved, waited, talking

1. We __moved__ close to my grandma's.
2. It took us the __longest__ time to get there.
3. I took my turn __driving__.
4. I said, "It's __taking__ us too long."
5. The streets are getting __wider__.
6. The __nicest__ part of this whole thing will be __talking__ to Grandma.
7. Mom __wanted__ a bigger house.
8. We saw my cousin. He __waved__ at us.
9. He __waited__ for us to come.
10. We were all __talking__ at once!

Language - Creative Writing.
Pretend you live in a tree house! Write a story describing what it's like to live in your tree house.

Answers will vary.

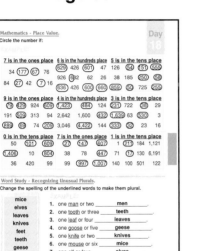

Page 71

Mathematics - Place Value.
Circle the number if:

7 is in the ones place / 6 is in the hundreds place / 5 is in the tens place

9 is in the ones place / 4 is in the hundreds place / 3 is in the tens place

0 is in the tens place / 7 is in the ones place / 1 is in the tens place

Word Study - Recognizing Unusual Plurals.
Change the spelling of the underlined words to make them plural.

mice, elves, leaves, knives, feet, teeth, geese, men

1. one man or two __men__
2. one tooth or three __teeth__
3. one leaf or four __leaves__
4. one goose or five __geese__
5. one knife or two __knives__
6. one mouse or six __mice__
7. one elf or four __elves__
8. one foot or nine __feet__

Page 72

Language - Writing Questions and Sentences Using Given Words.
Read the words in the word box. Then write three telling sentences and three question sentences. Use a word from the word box in each of your sentences.

Word Box: silence, attention, calmly, famous, honour, strange, moment, station, million, free, sniffed, shiver

1.
2.
3.
4.
5.
6.

Answers will vary.

Language - Adjectives.
Describing words. Words that describe tell something about other words in a sentence. Some words describe how things look. Some words describe how things sound. Some words describe how things feel or how things taste. Circle the describing words in these sentences.

1. Ella has on a pretty blue dress.
2. We left for our trip on a cloudy day.
3. The shrill whistle hurt my ears.
4. That sad child must be lost.
5. Joe likes a soft pillow.
6. The sour lemon made my mouth water.
7. Our class climbed a steep hill.
8. The door made a screechy noise.
9. The hot, wet sand felt good on our feet.
10. That fluffy yellow kitten is mine.

EXAMPLE:
The big, red wagon rolled down the hill.
Big and red are telling how the wagon looks.

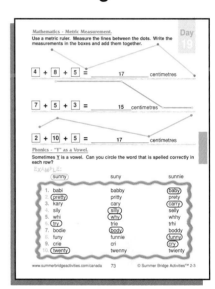

Page 73

Mathematics - Metric Measurement.
Use a metric ruler. Measure the lines between the dots. Write the measurements in the boxes and add them together.

4 + 8 + 5 = 17 centimetres

7 + 5 + 3 = 15 centimetres

2 + 10 + 5 = 17 centimetres

Phonics - "Y" as a Vowel.
Sometimes Y is a vowel. Can you circle the word that is spelled correctly in each row?

EXAMPLE: sunny / suny / sunnie

1. babi / babby / baby
2. pretty / pritty / prety
3. kary / cary / carry
4. sily / silly / selly
5. whi / why / whhy
6. try / trie / trhi
7. bodie / body / boddy
8. funy / funnie / funny
9. crie / cri / cry
10. twenty / twenny / twienty

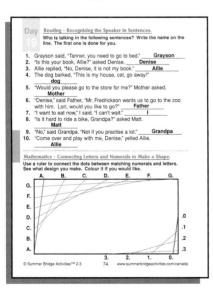

Page 74

Reading - Recognizing the Speaker in Sentences.
Who is talking in the following sentences? Write the name on the line. The first one is done for you.

1. Grayson said, "Tanner, you need to go to bed." __Grayson__
2. "Is this your book, Allie?" asked Denise. __Denise__
3. Allie replied, "No, Denise, it is not my book." __Allie__
4. The dog barked, "This is my house, cat, go away!" __dog__
5. "Would you please go to the store for me?" Mother asked. __Mother__
6. "Denise," said Father, "Mr. Fredrickson wants us to go to the zoo with him. Lori, would you like to go?" __Father__
7. "I want to eat now," I said. "I can't wait." __I__
8. "Is it hard to ride a bike, Grandpa?" asked Matt. __Matt__
9. "No," said Grandpa. "Not if you practise a lot." __Grandpa__
10. "Come over and play with me, Denise," yelled Allie. __Allie__

Mathematics - Connecting Letters and Numerals to Make a Shape.
Use a ruler to connect the dots between matching numerals and letters. See what design you make. Colour it if you would like.

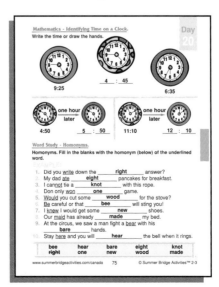

Page 75

Mathematics - Identifying Time on a Clock.
Write the time or draw the hands.

9:25 / 4:45 / 6:35

one hour later: 4:50 → 5:50
one hour later: 11:10 → 12:10

Word Study - Homonyms.
Homonyms. Fill in the blanks with the homonym (below) of the underlined word.

1. Did you write down the __right__ answer?
2. My dad ate __eight__ pancakes for breakfast.
3. I cannot tie a __knot__ with this rope.
4. Don only won __one__ game.
5. Would you cut some __wood__ for the stove?
6. Be careful or that __bee__ will sting you!
7. I knew I would get some __new__ shoes.
8. Our maid has already __made__ my bed.
9. At the circus, we saw a man fight a bear with his __bare__ hands.
10. Stay here and you will __hear__ the bell when it rings.

| bee | hear | bare | eight | knot |
| right | one | new | wood | made |

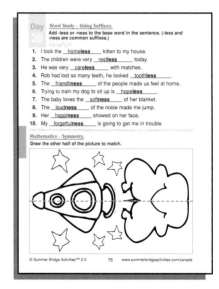

Page 76

Word Study - Using Suffixes.
Add -less or -ness to the base word in the sentence. (-less and -ness are common suffixes.)

1. I took the __homeless__ kitten to my house.
2. The children were very __restless__ today.
3. He was very __careless__ with matches.
4. Rob had lost so many teeth, he looked __toothless__.
5. The __friendliness__ of the people made us feel at home.
6. Trying to train my dog to sit up is __hopeless__.
7. The baby loves the __softness__ of her blanket.
8. The __loudness__ of the noise made me jump.
9. Her __happiness__ showed on her face.
10. My __forgetfulness__ is going to get me in trouble.

Mathematics - Symmetry.
Draw the other half of the picture to match.

Section 3

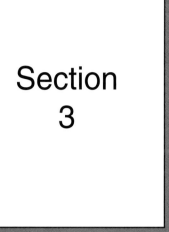

Mathematics - Using Symbols to Compare Quantities.
Write the signs for greater than (>), less than (<), or equal to (=) in the circles.

Day 1

7 + 7 (<) 15	9 + 7 (=) 16	8 + 9 (<) 18
8 + 6 (<) 14	13 - 4 (>) 10	10 - 4 (>) 6
15 (>) 1 + 9	16 + 4 (>) 17	17 - 9 (=) 8
3 + 3 (=) 2 + 4	11 (<) 3 + 9	4 (<) 12 - 8
8 + 9 (=) 9 + 8	5 + 8 (>) 6 + 7	15 - 5 (>) 13 - 4
11 - 4 (<) 6 + 2	12 - 6 (>) 6 + 6	18 - 8 (=) 8 + 8
12 - 1 (>) 12 - 6	10 + 1 (<) 4 + 7	9 + 3 (>) 14 - 7
3 (<) 13 - 5	5 + 9 (<) 16	14 - 8 (=) 5 + 1

Reading - Noting Detail.
Read the story. Complete the picture to go with the story.
Mary planted flowers in each pot. They grew fast. She put the flowers all in a row. The white flower was in the middle. The purple flower was second. The orange flower was not first. The yellow flower was last. Where was the pink flower? Where does the orange flower go?

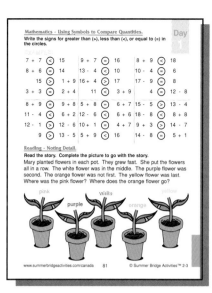

pink   white   yellow
    purple   orange

www.summerbridgeactivities.com/canada   81   © Summer Bridge Activities™ 2-3

Page 81

Day 1

Science - The Weather.
Weather is all around us. Sun, air, and water all work together to make different kinds of weather. Use the following words to write at least three weather sentences.

1. _____
2. _____ Answers will vary. _____
3. _____

clouds / rain / fog / flood / snowstorms / lightning / thunder / tornado / wind / sleet / hail / ice / sun

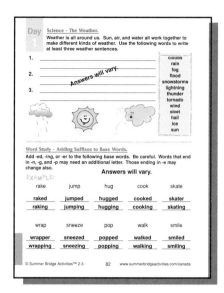

Word Study - Adding Suffixes to Base Words.
Add -ed, -ing, or -er to the following base words. Be careful. Words that end in -n, -g, and -p may need an additional letter. Those ending in -e may change also.

EXAMPLE:

Answers will vary.

rake	jump	hug	cook	skate
raked	jumped	hugged	cooked	skater
raking	jumping	hugging	cooking	skating
wrap	sneeze	pop	walk	smile
wrapper	sneezed	popped	walked	smiled
wrapping	sneezing	popping	walking	smiling

© Summer Bridge Activities™ 2-3   82   www.summerbridgeactivities.com/canada

Page 82

Mathematics - Metric Measurement.
Use a metric ruler. Find the length of each object.

Day 2

pencil	10 cm
comb	9 1/2 cm
pen	7 1/2 cm
nail	3 cm
worm	10 cm
toothbrush	12 1/2 cm
key	3 cm

Language - Verbs.
Doing words are called verbs. Some doing words mean to do it now or later; others mean we already did it. Put these doing words on the correct ladder.
EXAMPLE:

Do It			Did It
write	laughed	wore	wrote
wear	write	know	wore
fly	knew	flew	flew
know	blew	found	knew
blow	wear	blow	blew
find	wrote	find	found
laugh		fly	laughed

www.summerbridgeactivities.com/canada   83   © Summer Bridge Activities™ 2-3

Page 83

Day 2

Language - Capitalization and Punctuation.
Write these sentences correctly. Don't forget the capital letters, periods, question marks, commas, and quotation marks.

1. randy has five pets: a dog cat rabbit and two mice
Randy has five pets: a dog, cat, rabbit, and two mice.

2. do bluebirds eat seeds insects and plants
Do bluebirds eat seeds, insects, and plants?

3. would you please go to the store for me asked grayson
"Would you please go to the store for me?" asked Grayson.

4. my name is allie and i like candy
My name is Allie and I like candy.

Word Study - Classifying Antonyms, Homonyms and Synonyms.
Write the words under the correct heading.

	(opposite) Antonyms	(sound alike) Homonyms	(mean the same) Synonyms
would wood		would wood	
1. high low	high low		
2. pile heap			pile heap
3. weight wait		weight wait	
4. blend mix			blend mix
5. empty full	empty full		
6. difficult hard			difficult hard
7. rain reign		rain reign	
8. cool warm	cool warm		
9. crawl creep			crawl creep
10. groan grown		groan grown	

© Summer Bridge Activities™ 2-3   84   www.summerbridgeactivities.com/canada

Page 84

Mathematics - Fractions.
Colour in the correct fraction of each picture.

Day 3

= 100   = 10   = 1

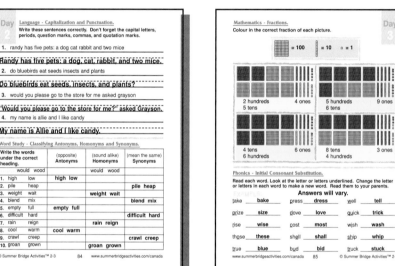

| 2 hundreds 5 tens | 4 ones | 5 hundreds 6 tens | 9 ones |
| 4 tens 6 hundreds | 6 ones | 8 tens 4 hundreds | 3 ones |

Phonics - Initial Consonant Substitution.
Read each word. Look at the letter or letters underlined. Change the letter or letters in each word to make a new word. Read them to your parents.
EXAMPLE:

Answers will vary.

take	bake	press	dress	well	tell
prize	size	dove	love	quick	trick
rise	wise	cost	most	wish	wash
those	these	shell	shall	ship	whip
true	blue	bud	bid	truck	stuck

© Summer Bridge Activities™ 2-3   85   © Summer Bridge Activities™ 2-3

Page 85

Day 3

Reading Sequence.
Read the story. Then number the events in the order they happened.

It had snowed for three days. When it stopped, the snow was so deep Tom and Don could not get out through the door of the cabin. The men had to climb out the upstairs window in order to get outside. They spent hours shoveling the snow away from the cabin door. At last, they were able to get the door open.

(2) The men climbed out the window.
(1) It snowed for three days.
(4) Don and Tom got the door open.
(3) The men shoveled snow for hours.

Language - Creativity.
Doors, Doors, Doors. There are many kinds of doors belonging to many interesting places and things: cars, houses, barns, bedrooms and basements.

Think of a door that could "lead" you to an interesting place or a strange thing. Draw a picture of your door and what's behind it.

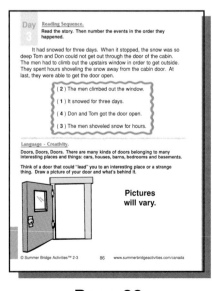

Pictures will vary.

© Summer Bridge Activities™ 2-3   86   www.summerbridgeactivities.com/canada

Page 86

Mathematics - Three Digit Subtraction.

Day 4

758	410	894	978	879	646
-126	-310	-251	-165	-704	-16
632	100	643	813	175	630

785	583	957	683	896	923
-223	-161	-140	-611	-840	-111
562	422	817	72	56	812

686	349	867	539	767	297
-255	-104	-36	-39	-10	-177
431	245	831	500	757	120

Language - Completing Analogies.
Words that go together. Write the correct word.
EXAMPLE:

1. Car is to road as boat is to _____lake_____
2. Cloud is to sky as worm is to _____ground_____
3. City is to buildings as forest is to _____trees_____
4. Knob is to door as pane is to _____window_____
5. Cub is to bear as calf is to _____cow_____
6. Bus is to car as airplane is to _____jet_____
7. Quack is to duck as meow is to _____cat_____
8. Begin is to start as end is to _____stop_____
9. Uncle is to aunt as father is to _____mother_____
10. Squirrel is to nut as cow is to _____hay_____

Word Bank
cat
ground
hay
window
mother
lake
trees
cow
jet
stop

© Summer Bridge Activities™ 2-3   87   © Summer Bridge Activities™ 2-3

Page 87

Day 4

Word Study - Spelling Words Correctly.
Finish writing the correct word in each sentence by changing the last letter and adding the correct ending.
EXAMPLE:

Word List
drier
happiest
easier
tried
carried
flies
worries
funniest

1. Wanda showed me the _funniest_ picture.
2. My clothes are _drier_ than yours.
3. That bird _flies_ south for the winter.
4. Joe _worries_ about his sick friend.
5. My book is _easier_ to read than yours.
6. This was my _happiest_ birthday ever!
7. Pete _carried_ his books to school.
8. I _tried_ to get the door unstuck.

Phonics - Word Families.
Find these -ack, -ick, -ock, -uck and -eck words in the word search puzzle. Circle them. Then fill in the blanks with words from the word box.

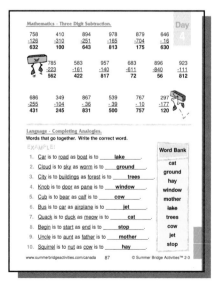

rock   duck   peck
wick   back   luck
lick   pack   sock
stuck speck wreck

The _____
put her _____
on the _____.

© Summer Bridge Activities™ 2-3   88   www.summerbridgeactivities.com/canada

Page 88

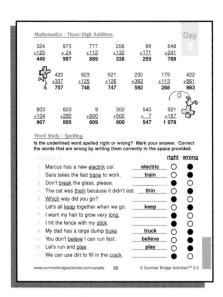

Page 89

Mathematics - Three-Digit Addition. Day 5

324	973	777	206	88	548
+125	+ 24	+112	+132	+171	+241
449	**997**	**889**	**338**	**259**	**789**
420	623	621	230	175	422
+337	+125	+126	+362	+113	+561
757	**748**	**747**	**592**	**288**	**983**
803	603	9	300	540	921
+104	+292	+600	+500	+ 7	+157
907	**895**	**609**	**800**	**547**	**1 078**

Word Study - Spelling.

Is the underlined word spelled right or wrong? Mark your answer. Correct the words that are wrong by writing them correctly in the space provided.

EXAMPLE:

		right	wrong
1. Marcus has a new electrik car.	**electric**	○	●
2. Sara takes the fast trane to work.	**train**	○	●
3. Don't break the glass, please.		●	○
4. The cat was thein because it didn't eat.	**thin**	○	●
5. Which way did you go?		●	○
6. Let's all keap together when we go.	**keep**	○	●
7. I want my hair to grow very long.		●	○
8. I hit the fence with my stick.		●	○
9. My dad has a large dump truke.	**truck**	○	●
10. You don't beleve I can run fast.	**believe**	○	●
11. Let's run and plae.	**play**	○	●
12. We can use dirt to fill in the crack.		●	○

www.summerbridgeactivities.com/canada 89 © Summer Bridge Activities™ 2-3

Page 89

Page 90

Day 5 **Reading - Context Clues.**

Read the story and fill in the blanks using the word list below.

cockatoos zoo you spray copy jump monkeys colourful lions zoo down

When you go to the **zoo**, you watch the animals, and they watch you. The elephants may **spray** you with water. The **monkeys** swing by their tails. They try to do what you do. Scratch your head, and they will **copy** you and do it, too. Jump up and **down**, and they will **jump**, too. My favorite animals at the zoo are the **lions**. My favorite birds are the **cockatoos**. They are bright and **colourful**. I love to go to the **zoo**! Don't **you**?

Reading Classification.

Write titles for the following lists. **Answers will vary.**

Birds	Sewing		
robin	needle	soap	milk
wren	thread	water	soda
blue jay	scissors	washcloth	water
canary	thimble	towel	juice

Water Animals	Wild Animals		
whale	lions	ice	mother
shark	tigers	snow	father
dolphin	bears	frost	sister
minnow	elephants	snowman	brother

© Summer Bridge Activities™ 2-3 90 www.summerbridgeactivities.com/canada

Page 90

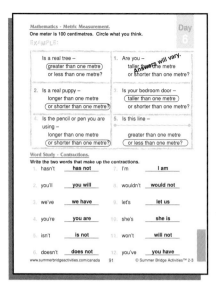

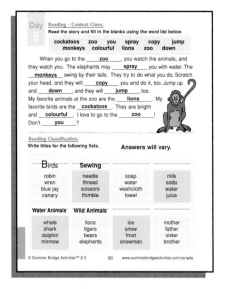

Page 91

Mathematics - Metric Measurement. Day 6

One meter is 100 centimetres. Circle what you think.

EXAMPLE:

Is a real tree – (greater than one metre) or less than one metre?	1. Are you – taller than one metre or shorter than one metre? **Answers will vary.**
2. Is a real puppy – longer than one metre (or shorter than one metre?)	3. Is your bedroom door – (taller than one metre) or shorter than one metre?
4. Is the pencil or pen you are using – longer than one metre (or shorter than one metre?)	5. Is this line – greater than one metre (or less than one metre?)

Word Study - Contractions.

Write the two words that make up the contractions.

1. hasn't	**has not**	7. I'm	**I am**
2. you'll	**you will**	8. wouldn't	**would not**
3. we've	**we have**	9. let's	**let us**
4. you're	**you are**	10. she's	**she is**
5. isn't	**is not**	11. won't	**will not**
6. doesn't	**does not**	12. you've	**you have**

www.summerbridgeactivities.com/canada 91 © Summer Bridge Activities™ 2-3

Page 91

Page 92

Day 6 **Reading.**

This does not make sense. You need to mark out all of the q's in each sentence. Then go back and read the story.

Greggqhadqaqbirthday.qHeqwantedqtoqinviteqallqofqhisq friendsqtoqhisqhouse.qHeqthoughtqthatqitqwouldqbeqfunqtoq haveqeveryoneqbringqtheirqswimmingqsuits.qTheyqcouldqrunq throughqtheqsprinklersqandqswimqinqhisqneighbor's qswimmingqpool.qHeqplannedqonqhavingqaqpizzaqandqiceqc ream.qEveryoneqcameqforqtheqparty.qTheyqateqandqswam.q Theyqlaughedqandqyelled.qTheyqplayedqgamesqandqwatch- edqvideosq.Everyoneqhadqaqsuperqtime.qGreggqalmostqforgot qtoqopenqhisqpresentsqbecauseqthereqwasqsoqmuchqtoq do!qHeqtoldqhisqmomqthatqmaybeqnextqyearqtheyqcould qhaveqhisqbirthdayqpartyqforqtwoqdaysqinsteadqofqone.

Language - Creative Writing.

It's your birthday. Blow out your candles and make a wish! Write about your wish and/or draw a picture about it.

Happy Birthday

Pictures will vary.

© Summer Bridge Activities™ 2-3 92 www.summerbridgeactivities.com/canada

Page 92

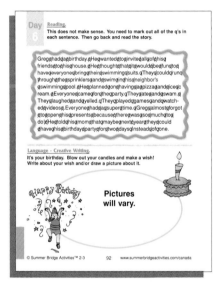

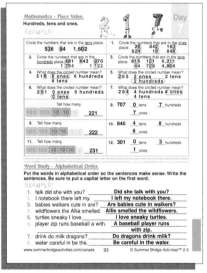

Page 93

Mathematics - Place Value. Day 7

Hundreds, tens and ones.

EXAMPLE:

Circle the numbers that are in the tens place. 5(3)6 (8)4 1,6(0)2	1. Circle the numbers that are in the ones place. 2(6) 84(2) 16(3) 92(4) 1(9) 84(6)
2. Circle the numbers that are in the hundreds place. (4)81 (6)43 (9)70 1 (2)94 1 (1)22	3. Circle the numbers that are in the tens place. 8(1)6 1(2)1 6,2(1)1 (4)4 7(2)9 4,8(6)4
4. What does the circled number mean? 51(6) (6 ones) 6 hundreds 6 tens	5. What does the circled number mean? (2)65 2 ones 2 tens (2 hundreds)
6. What does the circled number mean? 2(0)1 0 ones 0 hundreds (0 tens)	7. What does the circled number mean? 29(4) 4 hundreds (4 ones) 4 tens
EXAMPLE: Tell how many. 100 100 10 10 1 **221**	8. 707 **0** tens **7** hundreds **7** ones
9. Tell how many. 100 100 10 10 1 1 **222**	10. 846 **4** tens **8** hundreds **6** ones
11. Tell how many. 100 100 10 10 10 1 **231**	12. 301 **0** tens **3** hundreds **1** ones

Word Study - Alphabetical Order.

Put the words in alphabetical order so the sentences make sense. Write the sentences. Be sure to put a capital letter on the first word.

EXAMPLE:

1. talk did she with you? **Did she talk with you?**
2. I notebook there left my. **I left my notebook there.**
3. babies walkers cute in are? **Are babies cute in walkers?**
4. wildflowers the Allie smelled. **Allie smelled the wildflowers.**
5. turtles sneaky I love. **I love sneaky turtles.**
6. player zip runs baseball a with. **A baseball player runs with zip.**
7. drink do milk dragons? **Do dragons drink milk?**
8. water careful in be the. **Be careful in the water.**

www.summerbridgeactivities.com/canada 93 © Summer Bridge Activities™ 2-3

Page 93

Page 94

Day 7 **Reading - Recalling Events; Drawing Conclusions.**

Read the story and answer the questions.

Lori got up late today, so she missed the bus. She had to walk to school. She was tired and cranky when she got there. She promised herself that she would never sleep late again.

1. Why was Lori late for school?

She got up late.

2. Why did she have to walk?

She missed the bus.

3. What advice do you have for Lori?

Answers will vary.

Reading - Sequence Sentences in the Correct Order.

Let's make a sandwich. Number the sentences in the correct order. The first one has been done for you.

3 Put whatever else you like on your sandwich.

1 Take two pieces of bread. Put butter on top of each.

4 Put the two pieces of bread together.

2 Next put on the meat and cheese.

6 Eat your sandwich—yum, yum!

5 Cut the sandwich in two and put it on a plate.

7 Clean up after yourself.

© Summer Bridge Activities™ 2-3 94 www.summerbridgeactivities.com/canada

Page 94

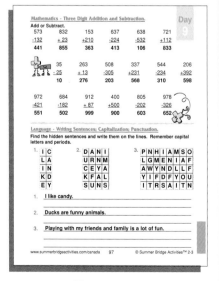

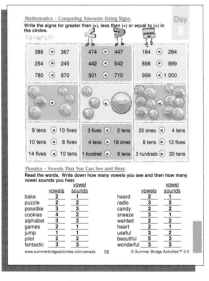

Page 95

Mathematics - Comparing Amounts Using Signs. Day 8

Write the signs for greater than (>), less than (<) or equal to (=) in the circles.

EXAMPLE:

386 (>) 367	474 (>) 447	184 (<) 284
254 (>) 245	442 (<) 542	898 (>) 889
780 (>) 870	501 (<) 710	999 (<) 1 000
(<)	(<)	(>)
9 tens (>) 10 fives	3 fives (<) 2 tens	25 ones (<) 4 tens
10 tens (>) 8 fives	4 tens (>) 18 ones	8 tens (>) 12 fives
14 fives (<) 10 tens	1 hundred (>) 6 tens	3 hundreds (>) 20 tens

Phonics - Vowels That You Can See and Hear.

Read the words. Write down how many vowels you see and then how many vowel sounds you hear.

	vowels	vowel sounds		vowels	vowel sounds
bake	2	1	heard	2	1
puzzle	2	2	radio	3	3
possible	3	3	candy	2	2
cookies	4	2	sneeze	3	1
alphabet	3	3	wanted	2	2
games	2	1	heart	2	1
jump	1	1	useful	3	2
pilot	2	2	beautiful	5	3
fantastic	3	3	wonderful	3	3

www.summerbridgeactivities.com/canada 95 © Summer Bridge Activities™ 2-3

Page 95

Page 96

Day 8 **Word Study - Antonyms.**

Antonyms are opposites. Read the sentences. Circle the word that will complete the sentence.

1. My shoes hurt my feet. They are too (little), big).
2. Be sure to (blame, (praise)) your friends when they do good work.
3. If you don't go now, I will not ((allow), refuse) you to go again.
4. Mother told me to wear (dirty, (clean)) clothes to the party.
5. Troy knows to take charge of the group. He is a very good (follower, (leader)).
6. When the light is red, you must remember to (go, (stop)).
7. The library is a place where we need to be (noisy, (quiet)).
8. The ((sour), sweet) pickle made my mouth feel strange.
9. The bread was so old, it became (fresh, (stale)).
10. While I'm gone, would you please ((answer), question) the phone?

big little

Reading - Following Written Directions.

Toucan Puffin Kingfisher

1. Colour the kingfisher's head and wings blue-green. Colour his breast red-orange. Leave his throat white. Colour his bill yellow-orange. Draw a post for him to stand on.
2. Colour the toucan's bill any three colours you wish. Colour his throat and breast orange. Colour around his eye green. Colour the rest of him black. Draw a branch for him to sit on.
3. Colour the puffin's bill green, red, and yellow. Leave his head and breast white. Colour the rest of him black, but not too dark. Draw some ice under the puffin's feet.
4. Colour all the birds' feet orange.

© Summer Bridge Activities™ 2-3 96 www.summerbridgeactivities.com/canada

Page 96

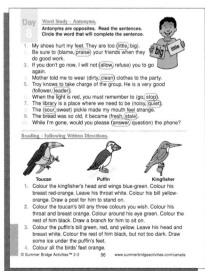

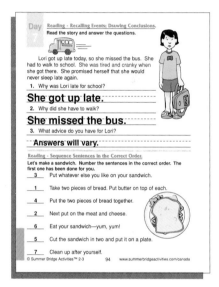

Page 97

Mathematics - Three Digit Addition and Subtraction. Day 9

Add or Subtract.

573	832	153	637	638	721
-132	+ 23	+210	-224	-532	+112
441	**855**	**363**	**413**	**106**	**833**
35	263	508	337	544	206
- 25	+ 13	-305	+231	-234	+392
10	**276**	**203**	**568**	**310**	**598**
972	684	912	400	805	978
-421	-182	+ 87	+500	-202	-326
551	**502**	**999**	**900**	**603**	**652**

Language - Writing Sentences; Capitalization; Punctuation.

Find the hidden sentences and write them on the lines. Remember capital letters and periods.

1.

I	C
L	A
I	N
K	D
E	Y

2.

D	A	N	I
U	R	N	M
C	E	Y	A
K	F	A	L
S	U	N	S

3.

P	N	H	I	A	M	S	O
L	G	M	E	N	I	A	F
A	W	Y	N	D	L	L	F
Y	I	F	D	F	Y	O	U
I	T	R	S	A	I	T	N

1. **I like candy.**
2. **Ducks are funny animals.**
3. **Playing with my friends and family is a lot of fun.**

www.summerbridgeactivities.com/canada 97 © Summer Bridge Activities™ 2-3

Page 97

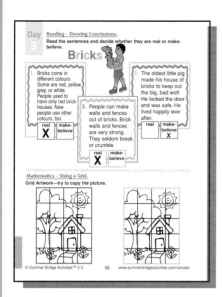

Page 98

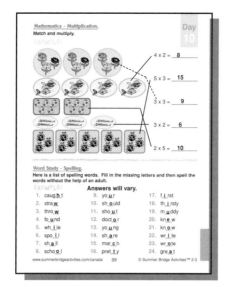

Page 99

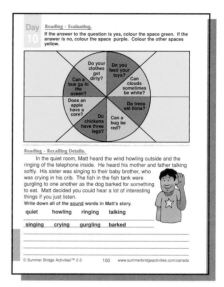

Page 100

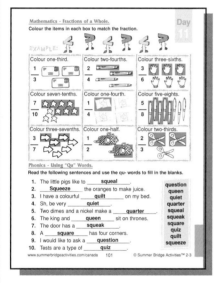

Page 101

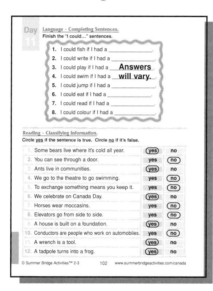

Page 102

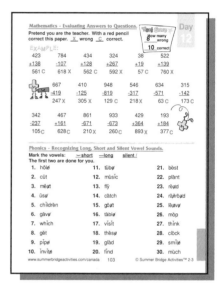

Page 103

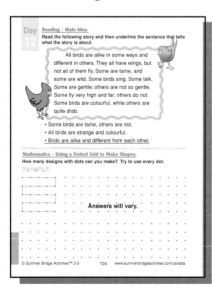

Page 104

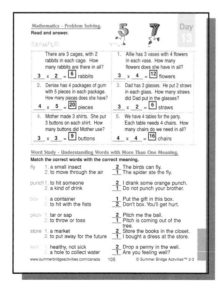

Page 105

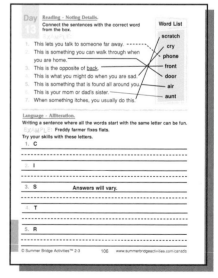

Page 106

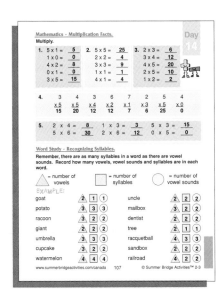

Page 107

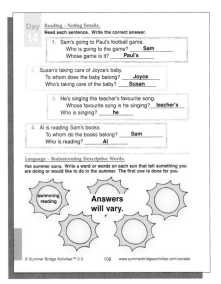

Page 108

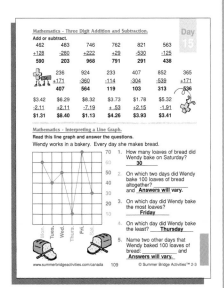

Page 109

Page 107

Multiply.

Day 14

1. 5 x 1 = **5**   2. 5 x 5 = **25**   3. 2 x 3 = **6**
   1 x 0 = **0**   2 x 2 = **4**   3 x 4 = **12**
   4 x 2 = **8**   3 x 3 = **9**   4 x 5 = **20**
   0 x 1 = **0**   1 x 1 = **1**   2 x 5 = **10**
   3 x 5 = **15**   4 x 1 = **4**   1 x 2 = **2**

4.
3	4	3	6	7	2	5	4
x 5	x 5	x 4	x 2	x 1	x 3	x 5	x 0
15	20	12	12	7	6	25	0

5. 2 x 4 = **8**   1 x 3 = **3**   5 x 3 = **15**
   5 x 6 = **30**   2 x 6 = **12**   0 x 5 = **0**

Word Study - Recognizing Syllables.
Remember, there are as many syllables in a word as there are vowel sounds. Record how many vowels, vowel sounds and syllables are in each word.

△ = number of vowels   □ = number of syllables   ○ = number of vowel sounds

EXAMPLE:
goat	△2 □1 ○1	uncle	△2 □2 ○2
potato	△3 □3 ○3	mailbox	△3 □2 ○2
racoon	△3 □2 ○2	dentist	△2 □2 ○2
giant	△2 □2 ○2	tree	△2 □1 ○1
umbrella	△3 □3 ○3	racquetball	△4 □3 ○3
cupcake	△3 □2 ○2	sandbox	△2 □2 ○2
watermelon	△4 □4 ○4	railroad	△4 □2 ○2

107

Page 108

Day 14

Read each sentence. Write the correct answer.

1. Sam's going to Paul's football game.
   Who is going to the game? **Sam**
   Whose game is it? **Paul's**

2. Susan's taking care of Joyce's baby.
   To whom does the baby belong? **Joyce**
   Who's taking care of the baby? **Susan**

3. He's singing the teacher's favourite song.
   Whose favourite song is he singing? **teacher's**
   Who is singing? **he**

4. Al is reading Sam's books.
   To whom do the books belong? **Sam**
   Who is reading? **Al**

Language - Brainstorming Descriptive Words.
Hot summer suns. Write a word or words on each sun that tell something you are doing or would like to do in the summer. The first one is done for you.

swimming reading

Answers will vary.

108

Page 109

Add or subtract.

Day 15

462	483	746	762	821	563
+128	-280	+222	+29	-530	-125
590	203	968	791	291	438

236	924	233	407	852	365
+171	-360	-114	-304	-539	+171
407	564	119	103	313	536

$3.42	$6.29	$8.32	$3.73	$1.78	$5.32
-2.11	+2.11	-7.19	+.53	+2.15	-1.91
$1.31	$8.40	$1.13	$4.26	$3.93	$3.41

Mathematics - Interpreting a Line Graph.
Read this line graph and answer the questions.
Wendy works in a bakery. Every day she makes bread.

1. How many loaves of bread did Wendy bake on Saturday? **30**
2. On which two days did Wendy bake 100 loaves of bread altogether? **Answers will vary.**
3. On which day did Wendy bake the most loaves? **Friday**
4. On which day did Wendy bake the least? **Thursday**
5. Name two other days that Wendy baked 100 loaves of bread: _____ and _____ **Answers will vary.**

109

Page 110

Day 16

Read the poem, and then do the activity below.

My Shadow
I have a little shadow that goes in and out with me,
And what can be the use of him is more than I can see.
He is very, very like me from the heels up to the head;
And I see him jump before me, when I jump into bed.
—Robert Louis Stevenson

1. What does your shadow do when you jump into bed?
jump before me
2. Who does your shadow look like?
very, very like me
3. When do you see your shadow?
sunny, lamp light, etc.
4. What else can your shadow do besides jump?
Answers will vary.

Language - Recognizing Complete and Incomplete Sentences.
Write yes if the sentence is complete, or no if it is not.

EXAMPLE:	A. Inside a large.	No
	B. Someone is walking on the sidewalk.	Yes
1.	Ted helped Jane.	Yes
2.	That road goes to.	No
3.	I went to a movie last night.	Yes
4.	We played in the park by.	No
5.	Who is going to?	No
6.	Today is my birthday.	Yes
7.	Under the swing in front of the house.	No
8.	Every Friday after school.	No
9.	Did you enjoy reading that book?	Yes
10.	Andy likes to play football.	Yes

110

Page 110

Better Bodies

Up until now, **Summer Bridge Activities**™ has been all about your mind . . .

But the other parts of you—who you are, how you act, and how you feel—are important, too. That's why this year we are introducing a whole new section in **Summer Bridge Activities**™: Building Better Bodies. These new pages are all about helping build a better you this summer.

Keeping your body strong and healthy helps you live better, learn better, and feel better. To keep your body healthy, you need to do things like eat right, get enough sleep, and exercise. The Building Better Bodies pages will teach you about good eating habits and the importance of proper exercise.

After a summer of Building Better Bodies and **Summer Bridge Activities**™, there may be a whole new you ready for school in the fall!

Foods I Need Each Day

2 meats, eggs, and nuts
6 breads, cereals, and grains
2 fruits
3 vegetables
2 milk and cheese

Draw or cut and paste pictures of the foods you need each day.

2 meats	2 fruits	2 milk

6 breads, cereals, and grains	3 vegetables

Meal Tracker

Keep a record of the servings you eat from each food group.
You can draw or write. Have an adult or friend do it, too; then, compare.

	Breads / Cereals	Milk	Meat	Fruits	Vegetables	Fats/ Sweets
Monday						
Tuesday						
Wednesday						
Thursday						
Friday						
Saturday						
Sunday						

	Breads / Cereals	Milk	Meat	Fruits	Vegetables	Fats/ Sweets
Monday						
Tuesday						
Wednesday						
Thursday						
Friday						
Saturday						
Sunday						

Nutrition

The food you eat helps your body grow and gives you energy to work and play. Some foods give you protein or fats. Other foods provide vitamins, minerals, or carbohydrates. These are all things your body needs. Eating a lots of different foods from the five major food groups every day can help you stay healthy.

Your body needs nutrients from each food group every day.

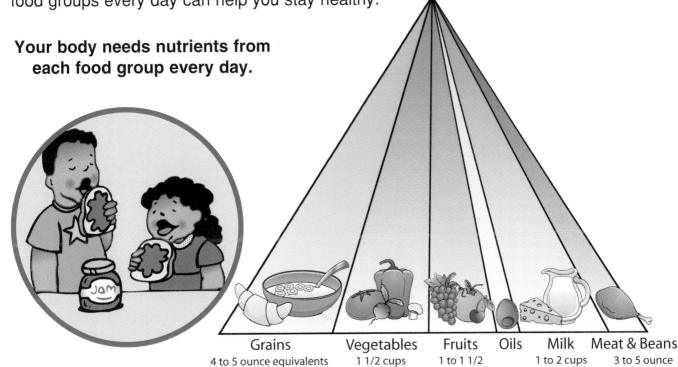

Grains	Vegetables	Fruits	Oils	Milk	Meat & Beans
4 to 5 ounce equivalents each day (an ounce might be a slice of bread, a packet of oatmeal, or a bowl of cereal)	1 1/2 cups each day	1 to 1 1/2 cups each day		1 to 2 cups of milk (or other calcium-rich food) each day	3 to 5 ounce equivalents each day

Put a ☐ around the four foods from the Grains Group.

Put a △ around the two foods from the Meat and Beans Group.

Put a ◇ around the three foods from the Milk Group.

Put a ○ around the two foods from the Fruits Group.

Put a ☐ around the four foods from the Vegetables Group.

Name _____   Date _____

How I Measure Up!

You will be filling out this page twice—once now and once at the end of the summer to see how you have grown. Have an adult help you measure yourself to fill in the blanks below.

around the neck ____

smile ____

neck to belly button ____

shoulder to elbow ____

around the wrist ____

elbow to wrist ____

around the waist ____

length of longest finger ____

waist to ankle ____

around the knee ____

around the ankle ____

foot length ____

around the neck ____

smile ____

neck to belly button ____

shoulder to elbow ____

around the waist ____

elbow to wrist ____

around the wrist ____

length of longest finger ____

waist to ankle ____

around the knee ____

around the ankle ____

foot length ____

Get Moving!

Did you know that getting no exercise can be almost as bad for you as smoking? So get moving this summer!

Summer is the perfect time to get out and get in shape. Your fitness program should include three parts:

Get 30 minutes of aerobic exercise per day, three to five days a week.

Exercise your muscles to improve strength and flexibility.

Make it FUN! Do things that you like to do. Include your friends and family.

Couch Potato Quiz

1. Name three things you do each day that get you moving.

2. Name three things you do a few times a week that are good exercise.

3. How many hours do you spend each week playing outside or exercising?

4. How much TV do you watch each day?

5. How much time do you spend playing computer or video games?

If the time you spend on activities 4 and 5 adds up to more than you spend on 1–3, you could be headed for a spud's life!

You can find information on exercise and fitness for kids at www.fitness.gov

Activity Pyramid

The Activity Pyramid works like the Food Pyramid. You can use the Activity Pyramid to help plan your summer exercise program. Fill in the blanks below.

List 1 thing that is not good exercise that you could do less of this summer.

1. _____

List 3 fun activities you enjoy that get you moving and are good exercise.

1. _____
2. _____
3. _____

List 3 activities you would like to do for aerobic exercise this summer.

1. _____
2. _____
3. _____

Cut Down On

TV time
video or computer games
sitting for more than
30 minutes at a time

2–3 Times a Week

Work & Play	Strength & Stretching
bowling	dancing
swinging	martial arts
fishing	gymnastics
jump rope	push-ups/pull-ups
yard work	

3–5 Times a Week
at least 20 minutes

Aerobic Exercise		Sports/Recreation	
walking	skating	soccer	relay races
running	bicycling	basketball	tennis
	swimming	volleyball	baseball

Every Day

walk
play outside
take the stairs

help with chores:
sweeping
washing dishes
picking up
clothes and toys

Adapted from the President's Council on Fitness and Sports

List 3 exercises you could do to build strength and flexibility this summer.

1. _____
2. _____
3. _____

List 2 sports you would like to participate in this summer.

1. _____
2. _____

List 5 everyday things you can do to get moving more often.

1. _____
2. _____
3. _____
4. _____
5. _____

Fitness Fundamentals

Physical fitness includes all of these things:

Cardiovascular Endurance. Your cardiovascular system includes your heart and blood vessels. You need a strong heart to pump your blood.

Muscular Strength. Strong muscles help us work, play, walk, and even stand.

Muscular Endurance. Endurance is how long you can use your muscles before they get tired.

Flexibility. Being flexible means you can stretch and bend easily.

The goal of your summer fitness program is to improve in all four areas of physical fitness.

You build cardiovascular endurance with **aerobic** exercise. For aerobic exercise, you need to use large muscle groups at a steady pace. This gets your heart pumping and makes you breathe faster to take in more oxygen. For aerobic exercise you can jog, walk, hike, swim, dance, ride a bike, climb stairs, rollerblade, and more. Exercises that work your muscles build **muscular strength** and **endurance**. Sit-ups, push-ups, and pull-ups work your muscles.

Most exercise will help you stay **flexible**. Try stretching your arms behind your neck while you walk, or bend and touch your toes while you watch TV.

You need at least 30 minutes of aerobic exercise per day, three to five days a week.

30:00

Draw a stick person. Give your person a heart (for aerobic exercise), muscles in the arms (for strength and endurance), and bent knees (for flexibility).

Your Summer Fitness Program

Start your summer fitness program by choosing at least one aerobic activity from your Activity Pyramid. You can choose more than one for variety. Write the activity below.

_____   _____   _____

Do this activity three to five times each week. Keep it up for at least 20 minutes each time. (Exercise hard enough to increase your heart rate and your breathing. But do not exercise so hard that you get dizzy or cannot catch your breath.)

Use this chart to plan when you will exercise or to record your activity after you exercise.

DATE	ACTIVITY	TIME

DATE	ACTIVITY	TIME

Plan a reward for meeting your exercise goals for two weeks.
(You can make copies of this chart to track your fitness all summer long.)

Start Slow!
Remember to start out slow. Exercise is about getting stronger. It's not about being superman or superwoman right off the bat.

Better Behaviour

For Parents: Introduction to Character Education

Character education is simply giving your child clear messages about the values you and your family consider important. Many studies have shown that a basic core of values is universal. You will find certain values reflected in the laws of every country and incorporated in the teachings of religious, ethical, and other belief systems throughout the world.

The character activities included here are designed to span the entire summer. Each week your child will be introduced to a new value, with a quote and two activities that illustrate it. Research has shown that character education is most effective when parents reinforce the values in their child's daily routine; therefore, we encourage parents to be involved as their child completes the lessons.

Here are some suggestions on how to maximize these lessons.

- Read through the lesson yourself. Then, set aside a block of time when you and your child can discuss the value.

- Plan a block of time to work on the suggested activities.

- Discuss the meaning of the quote with your child. Ask, "What do you think the quote means?" Have your child ask other members of the family the same question. If possible, include grandparents, aunts, uncles, and cousins.

- Use the quote as often as you can during the week. You'll be pleasantly surprised to learn that both you and your child will have it memorized.

- For extra motivation, you can set a reward for completing each week's activities.

- Point out to your child other people who are actively displaying a value.
  Example: "See how John is helping Mrs. Olsen by raking her leaves."

- Be sure to praise your child each time he practises a value. Example: "Mary, it was very courteous of you to wait until I finished speaking."

- Find time in your day to talk about values. Turn off the radio in the car and chat with your child; take a walk in the evening as a family; read a story about the weekly value at bedtime; or give a back rub while you talk about what makes your child happy or sad.

- Finally, model the values you want your child to acquire. Remember, children will do as you do, not as you say.

Respect

Respect is showing good manners toward all people, not just those you know or who are like you. Respect is treating everyone, male or female, rich or poor, no matter what religion, race, or culture, in a way that you would want to be treated.

The easiest way to do this is to decide to **never** take part in activities and to **never** use words that make fun of people because they are different from you or your friends.

Treat others as you would like to be treated.
~ The Golden Rule

Colour the picture below.

Activity

This week, go to the library and check out *Bein' with You This Way* by W. Nikola-Lisa (1995).

This book is a fun rap about things that make us different and things that make us the same. Read it with your parents!

Gratitude

Gratitude is when you thank people for the good things they have given you or done for you. Thinking about people and things in your life that make you feel thankful will help you become a happier person.

There are more than 465 different ways of saying thank you. Here are a few:

Danke   Toda   Merci   Gracias   Nandrí

Spasibo   Arigato   **Gadda ge**   Paldies   Hvala

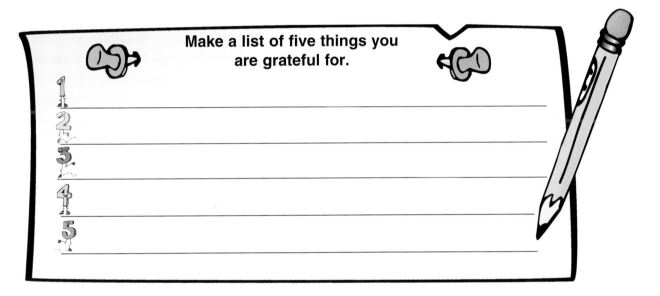

Make a list of five things you are grateful for.

1. _____
2. _____
3. _____
4. _____
5. _____

A Recipe for Saying Thanks

1. Make a colourful card.
2. On the inside, write a thank-you note to someone who has done something nice for you.
3. Address an envelope to that person.
4. Pick out a cool stamp.
5. Drop your note in the nearest mailbox.

Saying thank you creates love.

~ Daphne Rose Kingma

Manners

If you were the only person in the world, you would not have to have **good manners** or be **courteous**. However, there are more than 6 billion people on our planet, and good manners help us all get along with each other.

Children with good manners are usually well liked by other children and certainly by adults. Here are some simple rules for good manners:

- When you ask for something, say, "Please."
- When someone gives you something, say, "Thank you."
- When someone says, "Thank you", say, "You're welcome."
- If you walk in front of someone or bump into a person, say, "Excuse me."
- When someone else is talking, wait before speaking.
- Share and take turns.

No kindness, no matter how small, is ever wasted. ~ Aesop's Fables

See How I'm Nice

(sung to "Three Blind Mice")
See how I'm nice,
see how I'm nice.
Thanks, thanks, thanks.
Please, please, please.
I cover my nose whenever I
sneeze.
I sit on my chair, not on my knees.
I always say, "Thank you" when
I'm passed some peas.
Thanks, thanks, thanks.
Please, please, please.

I've Got Manners

Make a colourful poster to display on your bedroom door or on the refrigerator. List five ways you are going to practise your manners. Be creative and decorate with watercolors, poster paints, pictures cut from magazines, clip art, or geometric shapes.

Instead of making a poster, you could make a mobile to hang from your ceiling that shows five different manners to practise.

Choices

A **choice** is when you get to pick between two or more things. Often, one choice is better for you than another. Spend time thinking about which choice would be best for you before you make a decision.

Let's practise. Pick which you think is the best choice:

1. What might be best for you to eat?
   A. an apple   B. a candy bar   C. chips

2. What is a good time to go to bed on a school night?
   A. midnight   B. 8:00 P.M.   C. noon

3. If a friend pushes you, should you
   A. cry.   B. hit him/her.   C. tell your friend, in a nice voice, that you don't like being pushed.

Colour the picture below.

Activity

Go to the library and check out a copy of *The Tale of Peter Rabbit* by Beatrix Potter. Read it out loud with an adult. Talk about the choices Peter made during the story. Are there other choices that would have been better?

Friendship

Friends come in all sizes, shapes, and ages: brothers, sisters, parents, neighbours, good teachers, and school and sports friends.

There is a saying, "To have a friend you need to be a friend." Can you think of a day when someone might have tried to get you to say or do unkind things to someone else? Sometimes, you have to be brave to be a real friend.

Recipe for Friendship

1 cup of always listening to ideas and stories
2 pounds of never talking behind a friend's back
1 pound of no mean teasing
2 cups of always helping a friend who needs help

Take these ingredients and mix completely together. Add laughter, kindness, hugs, and even tears. Bake for as long as it takes to make your friendship good and strong.

It's so much more friendly with two.

~ A. A. Milne (creator of Winnie the Pooh)

Family Night at the Movies

Rent *Toy Story* or *Toy Story II*. Each movie is a simple, yet powerful, tale about true friendship. Fix a big bowl of popcorn to share with your family during the show.

International Friendship Day

The first Sunday in August is International Friendship Day. This is a perfect day to remember all of your friends and how they have helped you during your friendship. Give your friends a call or send them an email or a snail-mail

Confidence

People are **confident**, or have **confidence**, when they feel like they can succeed at a certain task. To feel confident about doing something, most people need to practise it over and over.

Reading, playing baseball, making a bed, writing in cursive, playing the flute, even mopping a floor are all examples of tasks that need to be practised before people feel confident they can succeed.

What are three things you feel confident doing? _____

_____

_____

What is one thing you want to feel more confident doing? _____

Make a plan for how and when you will practise until you feel confident.

_____

_____

You Crack Me Up!
Materials needed:
1 dozen eggs
a mixing bowl

Cracking eggs without breaking the yolk or getting egg whites all over your hands takes practise.

1. Watch an adult break an egg into the bowl. How did they hold their hands? How did they pull the egg apart?

2. Now, you try. Did you do a perfect job the first time? Keep trying until you begin to feel confident about cracking eggs.

3. Use the eggs immediately to make a cheese omelet or custard pie. Refrigerate any unused eggs for up to three days.

Determination

If at first you don't succeed,

try, try again.

~ Anonymous

Responsibility

You show **responsibility** by doing what you have agreed or promised to do. It might be a task, such as a homework assignment, or a chore, such as feeding your gerbil.

When you are young, your parents and teachers will give you simple tasks, like putting away toys or brushing your teeth without being asked. As you get older, you will be given more responsibility. You might be trusted to come home from a friend's house at a certain time or drive to the store for groceries.

It takes a lot of practise to grow up to be a responsible person. The easiest way to practise is by keeping your promises and doing what you know is right.

A parent is responsible for different things than a child or a teenager. Write three activities you are responsible for every day. Then, write three things a parent is responsible for every day.

If you want your eggs hatched, sit on them yourself. ~ Haitian Proverb

Activity

Materials needed:
21 pennies or counters such as beans, rocks, or marbles
2 small containers labeled #1 and #2

Decide on a reward for successfully completing this activity.
Put all the counters in container #1.
Review the three activities you are responsible for every day.

Each night before you go to bed, put one counter for each completed activity into container #2. At the end of seven days, count all of the counters in container #2.

If you have 16 or more counters in container #2, you are on your way to becoming very responsible. Collect your reward.

My reward is _____ .

Service/Helping

Service is **helping** another person or group of people without asking for any kind of reward or payment. These are some good things that happen when you do service:

1. You feel closer to the people in your community (neighbourhood).
2. You feel pride in yourself when you see that you can help other people in need.
3. Your family feels proud of you.
4. You will make new friends as you help others.

An old saying goes, "Charity begins at home." This means that you do not have to do big, important-sounding things to help people. You can start in your own home and neighbourhood.

Activity

Each day this week, do one act of service around your house. Don't ask for or take any kind of payment or reward. Be creative! Possible acts of service are:

1. Carry in the groceries, do the dishes, or fold the laundry.
2. Read aloud to a younger brother or sister.
3. Make breakfast or pack lunches.
4. Recycle newspapers and cans.
5. Clean the refrigerator or your room.

At the end of the week, think of a project to do with your family that will help your community. You could play musical instruments or sing at a nursing home, set up a lemonade stand and give the money you make to the Special Olympics, offer to play board games with children in hospital, or pick some flowers and take them to a neighbour. The list goes on and on.

Actions speak louder than words.
~ Anonymous

Colouring

Colour the picture below.

Honesty and Trust

Being an **honest** person means you do not steal, cheat, or tell lies. **Trust** is when you believe someone will be honest. If you are dishonest, or not truthful, people will not trust you.

You want to tell the truth because it is important to have your family and friends trust you. However, it takes courage to tell the truth, especially if you do not want people to get mad at you or be disappointed in the way you behaved.

How would your parents feel if you lied to them? People almost always find out about lies, and most parents will be angrier about a lie than if you had told the truth in the first place.

When family or friends ask about something, remember that honesty is telling the truth. Honesty is telling what really happened. Honesty is keeping your promises. *Be proud of being an honest person.*

Draw and colour a picture of yourself being honest.

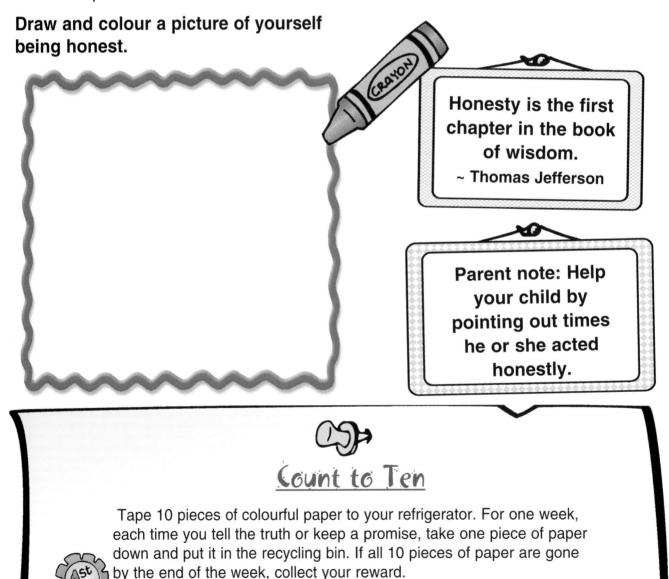

Honesty is the first chapter in the book of wisdom.
~ Thomas Jefferson

Parent note: Help your child by pointing out times he or she acted honestly.

Count to Ten

Tape 10 pieces of colourful paper to your refrigerator. For one week, each time you tell the truth or keep a promise, take one piece of paper down and put it in the recycling bin. If all 10 pieces of paper are gone by the end of the week, collect your reward.

My reward is _____

Happiness

Happiness is a feeling that comes when you enjoy your life. Different things make different people happy. Some people feel happy when they are playing soccer. Other people feel happy when they are playing the cello. It is important to understand what makes you happy so that you can include some of these things in your daily plan.

These are some actions that show you are happy: laughing, giggling, skipping, smiling, and hugging.

Make a list of five things that make you feel happy.

1. _____
2. _____
3. _____
4. _____
5. _____

Activity

Write down a plan to do one activity each day this week that makes you happy.

Try simple things—listen to your favourite song, play with a friend, bake muffins, shoot hoops, etc.

Be sure to thank everyone who helps you and do not forget to laugh!

Happy Thought

The world is so full

of a number of things,

I'm sure we should

all be happy as kings.

~Robert Louis Stevenson

Doodles

5 <u>Five things I'm</u>
<u>thankful for:</u>

1. _____
2. _____
3. _____
4. _____
5. _____

Notes

5 Five things I'm thankful for:

1. _____
2. _____
3. _____
4. _____
5. _____

Notes

Five things I'm thankful for:

1. _____
2. _____
3. _____
4. _____
5. _____

Addition and Subtraction (0-18)

Developing math skills can be a challenging experience for both parent and child.

- **Have a positive attitude.**
- **Relax and enjoy the learning process.**
- **Keep the learning time short and fun; you will get better results.**
- **Review the cards with your child.**
- **Read the front of the card.**
- **Check your answer on the reverse side.**
- **Separate those he does not know.**
- **Review those she does know.**
- **Gradually work through the other cards.**

These steps will help to build your child's confidence with addition and subtraction. Enjoy the rewards!

"Teacher, Teacher"

Three or more players.

Each player takes a turn as "Teacher."

The Teacher mixes up the flashcards and holds one card up at a time.

The first player to yell out "Teacher, Teacher," will have the first chance to give the answer.

If his answer is right he receives 5 points.

If her answer is wrong, she will not receive any points.

Move on to the next person until someone answers correctly.

Someone else is Teacher for the next round.

Repeat each round.

Reward the different levels; everyone wins!

Time Challenge

Follow the directions for "Teacher, Teacher," and add a time limit to it.

Increase the point system to meet the Time Challenge.

Reward the different levels; everyone wins!

2 + 1 **3** 9	2 + 2 **4** 8	3 + 1 **4** 9	3 + 2 **5** 10
3 + 3 **6** 8	4 + 1 **5** 9	4 + 2 **6** 7	4 + 3 **7** 8
4 + 4 **8** 8	5 + 1 **6** 9	5 + 2 **7** 6	5 + 3 **8** 7

$17 - 7 = 10$ 5	$17 - 8 = 9$ 4	$17 - 9 = 8$ 4	$16 - 7 = 9$ 3
$16 - 8 = 8$ 7	$16 - 9 = 7$ 6	$15 - 6 = 9$ 5	$15 - 7 = 8$ 6
$15 - 8 = 7$ 8	$15 - 9 = 6$ 7	$14 - 5 = 9$ 6	$14 - 6 = 8$ 8

5 + 4 ___ 9	5 + 5 ___ 10	6 + 1 ___ 7	6 + 2 ___ 8
9	5	6	7
6 + 3 ___ 9	6 + 4 ___ 10	6 + 5 ___ 11	6 + 6 ___ 12
5	6	7	8
7 + 1 ___ 8	7 + 2 ___ 9	7 + 3 ___ 10	7 + 4 ___ 11
7	8	9	4

$$14 - 7 = 7$$

8

$$14 - 8 = 6$$

7

$$14 - 9 = 5$$

10

$$13 - 4 = 9$$

9

$$13 - 5 = 8$$

12

$$13 - 6 = 7$$

11

$$13 - 7 = 6$$

10

$$13 - 8 = 5$$

9

$$13 - 9 = 4$$

11

$$12 - 3 = 9$$

10

$$12 - 4 = 8$$

9

$$12 - 5 = 7$$

8

7 + 5 **12**	7 + 6 **13**	7 + 7 **14**	8 + 1 **9**
3	4	5	6
8 + 2 **10**	8 + 3 **11**	8 + 4 **12**	8 + 5 **13**
7	8	9	10
8 + 6 **14**	8 + 7 **15**	8 + 8 **16**	9 + 1 **10**
3	4	5	6

12 − 6 ___ 6	12 − 7 ___ 5	12 − 8 ___ 4	12 − 9 ___ 3
9	14	13	12
11 − 1 ___ 10	11 − 2 ___ 9	11 − 3 ___ 8	11 − 4 ___ 7
13	12	11	10
11 − 5 ___ 6	11 − 6 ___ 5	11 − 7 ___ 4	11 − 8 ___ 3
10	16	15	14

9	9	9	9
+ 2	+ 3	+ 4	+ 5
11	12	13	14
7	8	9	2

9	9	9	9
+ 6	+ 7	+ 8	+ 9
15	16	17	18
3	4	5	6

10	10	10	10
+ 1	+ 2	+ 3	+ 4
11	12	13	14
7	8	1	2

$\begin{array}{r} 11 \\ -\ 9 \\ \hline 2 \end{array}$	$\begin{array}{r} 10 \\ -\ 1 \\ \hline 9 \end{array}$	$\begin{array}{r} 10 \\ -\ 2 \\ \hline 8 \end{array}$	$\begin{array}{r} 10 \\ -\ 3 \\ \hline 7 \end{array}$
14	13	12	11
$\begin{array}{r} 10 \\ -\ 4 \\ \hline 6 \end{array}$	$\begin{array}{r} 10 \\ -\ 5 \\ \hline 5 \end{array}$	$\begin{array}{r} 10 \\ -\ 6 \\ \hline 4 \end{array}$	$\begin{array}{r} 10 \\ -\ 7 \\ \hline 3 \end{array}$
18	17	16	15
$\begin{array}{r} 10 \\ -\ 8 \\ \hline 2 \end{array}$	$\begin{array}{r} 10 \\ -\ 9 \\ \hline 1 \end{array}$	$\begin{array}{r} 9 \\ -\ 1 \\ \hline 8 \end{array}$	$\begin{array}{r} 9 \\ -\ 2 \\ \hline 7 \end{array}$
14	13	12	11

10 + 5 ――― 15	10 + 6 ――― 16	10 + 7 ――― 17	10 + 8 ――― 18
3	4	5	6
11 + 1 ――― 12	11 + 2 ――― 13	11 + 3 ――― 14	11 + 4 ――― 15
6	7	1	2
11 + 5 ――― 16	11 + 6 ――― 17	11 + 7 ――― 18	12 + 1 ――― 13
2	3	4	5

9 − 3	9 − 4	9 − 5	9 − 6
18	17	16	15
9 − 7	9 − 8	8 − 1	8 − 2
15	14	13	12
8 − 3	8 − 4	8 − 5	8 − 6
13	18	17	16

12 + 2	12 + 3	12 + 4	12 + 5
4	5	6	1
12 + 6	13 + 2	13 + 3	13 + 4
0	1	2	3
13 + 5	14 + 1	14 + 2	14 + 3
2	3	4	5

8 − 7 17	7 − 1 16	7 − 2 15	7 − 3 14
7 − 4 17	7 − 5 16	7 − 6 15	7 − 7 18
6 − 1 17	6 − 2 16	6 − 3 15	6 − 4 18

14 + 4 2	15 + 1 3	15 + 2 4	15 + 3 1
16 + 1 1	16 + 2 2	17 + 1 3	18 -12 1
18 -11 1	18 -10 1	18 - 9 2	18 - 8 0

6	5	5	5
− 5	− 1	− 2	− 3
18	17	16	18

5	4	4	4
− 4	− 1	− 2	− 3
6	18	18	17

4	3	3	2
− 4	− 1	− 2	− 1
10	9	8	7

-Nice Work- You've Hit Your Goal!

your name

has completed Summer Bridge Activities ™

Ms. Hansen

Ms. Hansen

Parent's Signature

Mr. Fredrickson

Mr. Fredrickson

www.summerbridgeactivities.com